This is the first study of William Collins that makes use of material discovered recently among the Warton papers at Oxford University. It not only investigates the life and work of the man whose "Ode to Evening" remains possibly the greatest herald of the Romantic movement, but explores the ways in which his poetry was appreciated by the eighteenth-century reader which differ from those of the reader today.

By showing how our entire grasp of personification has so changed that long-accepted responses to eighteenth-century poetry must be altered, Professor Sigworth clears away many misleading post-Romantic apprehensions. Such major poets as Dryden and Pope, heretofore thought thoroughly evaluated, are cast in a new light by this study.

William Collins' brief life and small, uneven production stand at a crucial turning point in English literature. No attempt is made here to present him as a major figure, but he does emerge as a poet of unique accomplishment whose reappraisal clarifies our entire understanding of eighteenth-century poetry.

awarded his B.A., M.A., an[d] ... from the University of Ca[lifornia at Ber]keley. In 1955-56 he was in [...] on a Ford Fellowship, where [...] tensive studies in the taste an[d ...] of the eighteenth century.

Professor Sigworth's *Four Si[yl]es of a Decade, 1740-1750,* was published by the New York Public Library in 1960. *William Collins* was recently completed during a second stay in Britain. He is also the author of a book on the late eighteenth-century poet George Crabbe, which will be published soon. Professor Sigworth has read papers before the Modern Language Association, and he was chairman of the English II section of the Philological Association of the Pacific Coast.

Twayne's English Authors Series

Sylvia E. Bowman, *Editor*

INDIANA UNIVERSITY

William Collins

TEAS 25

William Collins

By OLIVER F. SIGWORTH

University of Arizona

Twayne Publishers, Inc.   ::   New York

Library of Congress Catalog Card Number: 65–18226

This book is for
HEATHER

Preface

The aim of this little book is to be a guide to the appreciation of the poetry of William Collins and, incidentally, to the appreciation of a certain kind of eighteenth-century poetry the possible pleasures of which are today ordinarily overlooked. It is also the first extended study of Collins to make use of the new material discovered among the Warton papers at Oxford and published under the editorship of Mr. J. S. Cunningham. These *Drafts and Fragments* by Collins are interesting enough to demand more detailed examination than the limits of this book allowed, but they are not in themselves justification for my study, the hope of which is to induce a few people to look at Collins and the poetry of the 1740's with a fresher eye and to listen with a keener ear.

It is no longer necessary to argue the case for Dryden, Pope, and Johnson against the Romantics and Victorians. Their kind of eighteenth-century poetry has again come into its own, and most readers will recognize its value even though it is no longer our sort of poetry—perhaps *because* it is no longer our sort of poetry: that is (willfully ignoring most of the twentieth century), the sort of poetry most commonly written in English since 1800. On the other hand, while most of Collins' poetry, as well as Gray's, has been ignored, a few poems have been generally anthologized and presumably loved because they seemed to be our sort of poetry, even though they are not. There is a case for Collins' lesser-known verse which has not been argued, and which is powerfully supported by recent investigations into eighteenth-century poetics, particularly by those inquiring into the use of personifications and into the concept of "correctness." It is, principally, a point of view arising out of these investigations which my book presents.

In making my case I have not hesitated to apply to a single

poet what has already been done for a whole period. My notes indicate my indebtedness to scholarship: to the works by Carver and Ainsworth on Collins, and particularly to those by Professors Bertrand H. Bronson, Earl R. Wasserman, George N. Shuster, and others on eighteenth-century poetics. If my case is a good one, the credit is theirs as much as mine.

I am grateful to the University of Arizona for granting me a sabbatical leave during which I wrote this book, and to the Clarendon Press and the President and Fellows of Trinity College, Oxford, for permission to quote extensively from *William Collins: Drafts and Fragments of Verse*. I must also thank Patrick J. McCarthy for special assistance under extraordinary circumstances, and Mr. William Ven Rooy for preparing the index.

OLIVER F. SIGWORTH

London, Tucson
1962-63

Contents

Preface

Chronology

1. "No Common Loss"   17

2. The Poetry and the Age   57

3. The Poems Themselves   87

4. Collins as Poet   145

Notes and References   167

Selected Bibliography   179

Index   187

Chronology

1721 William Collins born about Christmas at Chichester, son of William Collins, hatter and mayor of Chichester for the second time. The mayor was forty-seven, his wife forty, and two daughters were seventeen and sixteen.

1721– No definite information about Collins' very early life.
1733 Possibly he attended the Prebendal School, Chichester.

1733 Admitted as a scholar on the foundation of Winchester College, where he met Joseph Warton. Father died.

1738 First publication (?), verses "On Hercules" in *Gentleman's Magazine*.

1739 First authenticated publication, "Sonnet" ("When *Phœbe* form'd a wanton smile"), *Gentleman's Magazine* for October. During his later years at Winchester wrote *Persian Eclogues*.

1740 March 21, admitted as Commoner of Queens College, Oxford. During the summer placed first upon the roll of students to be received in succession at New College, but no vacancy occurred.

1741 July 29, elected to a Demyship at Magdalen College, probably through the influence of a much older cousin, William Payne.

1742 January, publication of *Persian Eclogues*.

1743 November 18, received the Bachelor of Arts from Oxford. Anonymous publication of *Verses Humbly Address'd to Sir Thomas Hanmer*.

1744 *An Epistle: Addrest to Sir Thomas Hanmer* and *A Song from the "Cymbelyne"* published in the same folio. July, Collins' mother died, her will directed that her property be sold and the proceeds divided equally between the three children. (The will was not proved until August 12, 1745.)

Collins resigned Demyship and left Oxford for London, where Mulso saw him in July. Collins applied to Duke of Richmond for curacy. In October, a neighbor of Mulso in Soho. Probably engaged to write lives for *Biographia Britannica.* In December *A Literary Journal* (Dublin) put at the head of a list of books deserving mention "A Review of the Advancement of Learning from 1300 to 1521 by Wm Collins, 4to."

1745   Early in the year Collins' uncle, Charles Collins, died, making William his heir (the will proved March 5), though the provisions were not to take effect until one year after death. In spring or early summer Collins pursued by bailiffs, met Johnson, escaped into country near Richmond, where he met Thomson. In summer visited his uncle Colonel Martin in Flanders.

1746   April 10, mortgaged property in Chichester; May 30, sold property. April 16, Battle of Culloden. In May, visited Guildford races, met Joseph Warton, made abortive plans for joint publication of odes. In July, again in Flanders, though his uncle was in Scotland. December, publication of *Odes on Several Descriptive and Allegoric Subjects.*

1747   Disposed of property in Chichester owned jointly with sisters. Essay by Collins (?) published in Dodsley's *Museum.* Project of "Clarendon Review" with John Gilbert Cooper. Probably first met John Home.

1748   "Ode to Evening" and "Colonel Ross" reprinted in Dodsley's *Collection.* August 27, Thomson died.

1749   Colonel Martin died, probably left no substantial estate. June, *Ode Occasion'd by the Death of Mr. Thomson* published. October, Collins and sisters provided for disposal of estate inherited from Alderman Collins. Collins met Barrow; began composing "Popular Superstitions." Bought back and burned remaining copies of *Odes.*

1750   February and March, announcements of forthcoming "Epistle to the Editor of Fairfax . . ." July 2, "The Passions" performed at Oxford. First illness.

1751   Easter, very ill, but recovered by June. Probably in this year he retired more or less permanently to Chichester.

1754   Visited Warton in Oxford. Confined for a short time to a madhouse in Chelsea (?). Returned to Chichester to live rest of life with his sister, Anne Sempill.

1757 *Persian Eclogues* reissued, slightly altered, as *Oriental Eclogues*.

1759 June 12, Collins dies.

1763 First collected edition of Collins' poems in *Poetical Calendar*.

William Collins

CHAPTER 1

"No Common Loss"

IN 1754 Gilbert White saw William Collins at Oxford "under the Merton Wall, in a very affecting situation, struggling, and conveyed by force, in the arms of two or three men, towards the parish of St. Clement, in which was a house that took in such unhappy objects." [1] Collins had come to Oxford to pay a visit to his friend Thomas Warton, but his rather mysterious mortal sickness was upon him, affecting both his mind and his body to the extent that he had upon another occasion not the strength to drag himself unassisted from his lodgings to Warton's rooms in Trinity College. He died five years later at his sister's house in Chichester, virtually forgotten by the very small public he had found and, according to some reports, mistreated by his only near relative.

It is easy to make too much of the irony of the situation. Collins had been that one eighteenth-century poet about whom Hazlitt was to say, "He is the only one of the minor poets of whom, if he had lived, it cannot be said that he might not have done the greatest things." [2] His fame during his lifetime was negligible, yet some of those who knew his poems were fervent in their admiration. Thirty years after his death he was admitted into collections as a "standard author," and there, largely on the strength of two or three poems of unparalleled artistry, he has safely remained. And now, more than two hundred years after his unnoticed death, there is a small shelf of books *about* the man whose fame rests upon an achievement counted in pages, not in volumes, who died mad [3] and forgotten by all but a few friends.

The point is the way in which he was remembered, and by whom. He was remembered by, among others, Samuel Johnson, who in 1763 wrote the first memoir of Collins, who was Collins' friend, but who seems not to have known quite what to make of him. He was also remembered by Francis Fawkes and William

Woty who, in the *Poetical Calendar* for 1763, printed Johnson's little biography together with most of Collins' poems—the first "edition" of the poet.[4] Johnson did not think very highly of Collins' poetry, but loved the man; but Goldsmith, who was not acquainted with the man, cordially recommended the weakest of his poetry. There were some, though, like John Langhorne, whose enthusiasm for the poetry knew no reasonable bounds, and whose encomiastic edition of 1765 may actually have retarded Collins' more general reputation by the very excess of its praise.

He was remembered also by the brothers Joseph and Thomas Warton, who exerted themselves very little, to be sure, in perpetuating Collins' memory. Thomas, in his *History of English Poetry*, pays Collins several pleasant compliments, but what we may regret is that Joseph, who was at one time Collins' particular friend, did not set down what he remembered of their youthful days at Winchester. Interest in biographical writing was growing during the eighteenth century, and it is therefore an intriguing fact that so little should be known about Collins and that Joseph Warton, who was, after all, something of a scholar, should not have thought it worth his while to record his unique impressions of a poet whom we now consider to have occupied a central, if small, place in the literature of his age. Probably it did not seriously occur to Joseph that anyone would be more interested in Collins than in James Hammond, for example, now utterly forgotten except for the tenuous fame conferred by Johnson's scarcely complimentary and very brief "Life," but whose *Elegies* were bound with Collins' poems in Bell's pocket edition of the English poets.[5] Nor was Joseph aware that the twentieth century might be particularly interested in searching out in Collins' early years a clue to the calamity of his later life. To the eighteenth century his madness was "an excess of enthusiasm," with a dark hint that just perhaps he ended no better than he deserved for having "loved fairies, genii, giants, and monsters" and for desiring to attain "the grandeur of wildness, and the novelty of extravagance" [6] in his verse.

I   *Chichester and Winchester*

We can discover, therefore, very little about Collins' early life. He was born at Chichester in Sussex probably just before Christmas, 1721.[7] He was baptized on New Year's Day, 1722. His early years must have been those of the favored child of comfortable bourgeoisie, for he was the third child and only son of William Collins, hatter, and in 1721 for the second time the mayor of Chichester. At the time of his son's birth the elder Collins was forty-seven years old and his wife forty; their two daughters, Elizabeth and Anne, were, respectively, seventeen and sixteen years older than their only brother. The fact that the future poet was an only child in a household of adults, that he may have had, in effect, three mothers, is worth noting, particularly when we consider that the Collins household, though not wealthy, was clearly in a position to pamper a child.

That the elder Collins was a substantial citizen is confirmed not only by his election to civic office but also by the fact that in 1715 he took a nine-year lease, for which he paid two hundred pounds and a yearly rent of five shillings, on "pens used for hogs, sheep, and lambs, which are moveable, and extend the whole length of the East and part of the North Streets." [8] Although by trade a hatter, who by 1720 had grown into a haberdasher,[9] Alderman Collins seems to have wanted to profit by one of the chief enterprises of Chichester at the time, supplying the navy at nearby Portsmouth. The pens were the property of Chichester Corporation, and we need not assume that Collins himself traded in livestock, but only that he recovered a profit from letting the pens for short terms to those who fattened the animals for slaughter. Public records again yield the name of the elder Collins in 1727 in connection with financial transactions leading to litigation in that year and again in 1730 to recover the value of tithes due him as sub-lessor of some property in Chichester.

The Collins family, then, was no doubt in a position to provide the best education available for William. Most writers have assumed that young William attended the Prebendal Free School, Chichester, but Mr. Carver points out that this school was a "charitable foundation for the benefit of a limited number of children whose parents could not afford the cost of education; and it is equally unlikely that an alderman and former mayor would have allowed his son to be nominated in competition with the genuinely poor and that, if the nomination had been proposed, the trustees would have approved the election." [10] This argument is reasonable enough, but the case is not quite so clear. According to the terms of its foundation in 1479, the school was to serve "as a nursery for the clergy, and the education of all born within the diocese . . ." [11] Just how many of the "genuinely poor" it would have occurred to anyone in the early 1700's to nominate for a vacancy, or, for that matter, how many of these poor could have been considered suitable to be placed in a "nursery for the clergy," is by no means certain. Very possibly none. It is true that the master was forbidden to accept gratuities from the parents, but it is not impossible that a contribution to the Cathedral Chapter would have been accepted, and that, if the education offered at the Prebendal School were of a quality to attract the notice of a former mayor, he might have contrived to send his son there, particularly if that son were, as seems possible considering the family's clerical connections,[12] designed for the clergy. Moy Thomas records it as "a tradition" that Collins attended the school,[13] but how firm the tradition was we cannot now say. The matter is not of great importance, and can never be certainly settled since the school at that time did not keep records.

Whether the boy attended a school or, as Mr. Carver suggests, learned his first letters at home or under the tutelage of a local curate, he was well enough prepared by the time he was eleven to be admitted as a scholar to Winchester College, where the College register bears the notation "Gulielm^s Collins de Chichester, Com. Sussex, Adm. 19 Jan., 1733"—the year, incidentally, in which his father died. "In this venerable institution," says Moy Thomas, "where the scholars on the foundation wear the dress prescribed by the rules of the founder, in which rejoicings over a holiday are sung in ancient Latin verse, and terms and phrases long fallen into disuse without its wall are still the current talk of healthy boys, Collins remained seven years." [14]

Certainly we are safe in saying that Collins' years at Winchester were exceedingly important, no doubt crucial. It was here that he made friendships, with Joseph Warton particularly, but also with William Whitehead, the future Poet Laureate; James Hampton, translator of Polybius; and John Mulso, whom we will encounter later in this narrative. It was here that he studied mythology and legend in the language of Homer and Virgil, a study which, judging from his later poetry, we can only think must have appealed both to the boy of eleven who entered the school and to the young man of eighteen who left it. Here he read Shakespeare, as we have reason to believe from the one remembered line of a poem "On the Battle of the Schoolbooks," written, tradition has it, when he was twelve: "And every Gradus flapped his leathern wing." "Leathern wing" comes from *A Midsummer Night's Dream,* "Some war with rere-mice for their leathern wings / To make my small elves coats" (II, ii, 4-5), and it reappears later in "Ode to Evening."

And it was at Winchester also that he not only wrote but published his first poems. Something must be said particularly of the friendships and the early poems; the two go together, for the first authenticated poem by Collins appeared in the *Gentleman's Magazine* for October, 1739, together with poems sent in the same packet by two of his schoolfellows, one of whom was Joseph Warton.

The association between Collins and the Wartons is no doubt extremely worth investigation for anyone concerned with Collins' poetry.[15] When we say "the Wartons," however, we too often refer only to the brothers, and overlook Thomas the elder, who may certainly be relevant to our present concern with Collins. There is no reason to believe that the Collins family had any particularly literary bent, or that Collins himself had displayed such interests before he left for Winchester. It would not have been extraordinary for such inclinations to have manifested themselves and been noted by the time Collins was eleven. Yet it was while he was at Winchester, and after he had met Joseph Warton, who was only a few months younger than Collins but who entered Winchester two years later, that his talents first manifested themselves. Speculation is dangerous, but Collins' talents developed so clearly in a way heralded in some of the interests displayed by the elder Warton and by Joseph, and later on by Thomas the younger, that we cannot resist inferring that an influence was at work unlikely, so far as we can tell, to be accounted for in terms of the curriculum at Winchester. The Warton family was thoroughly literary, and it is possible that the example of Joseph first persuaded the youth from the Chichester hatter's household that literary interests were possible, so to speak. And the poems of the elder Warton show a certain kind of literary interest which pretty clearly was transmitted to and developed by his sons—and in a much more remarkable way by Collins.

I shall have occasion in a few pages to speak in a very special sense of Collins' "rebellion," and I do not want to confuse my arguments or to mislead my readers by implying that the very mild and genteel ways in which Thomas Warton the Elder differed from his poetic contemporaries were "rebellious," or even, really, that he differed very much from his contemporaries. What I want to make clear is that I believe there is a very tenuous connection—one shimmering like a ray of light rather than binding like a cord, but nonetheless there—between Collins at Oxford and Collins after Oxford and the actions which have puzzled some of his biographers—a connection between the Collins of 1745, not to speak of the Collins of the great odes, and what Joseph may have brought to Winchester of the elder Warton's attitudes and interests. And since, particularly at this early stage in his career, Collins' life and work cannot very readily be separated, I should like to digress for a few words about Collins and the Wartons at this point rather than postpone discussing this influence until a later chapter where, perhaps, it more logically belongs.

Thomas Senior was not a very good poet—and he was reputed to have been a not very good Professor of Poetry at Oxford—yet the little volume of his poems piously gathered together and published by Joseph in 1748, three years after his father's death, is not without attractive qualities. There is nothing in the volume either unbearably pompous or embarrassingly facetious—a negative recommendation which would not apply to most very minor poetry at any time and particularly not to most of that produced in the first half of the eighteenth century. Several conventional epistles in heroic couplets appear, and translations from Latin and Biblical paraphrases in the same measure; but there are also translations in a blank verse which avoids the inflated doughiness of some of the Miltonic imitators. There are Odes in various measures, including an "Ode Written in a Grotto near Farnham in Surry, call'd Ludlow's Cave," a couple of stanzas of which may be worth quoting:

II

The Nymphs that keep this circling Wood,
And beauteous *Naïads* of the neighb'ring Flood
  With their Dew-dropping Hair,
Oft to this unadorned Cave repair,
  To dance and trip it in a Round
  On the smooth and Hallow'd Ground;
And say—"That *Dian*'s Grott, and *Thetis*' Bow'rs,
"Must yield in Coolness and in Shade to our's."—

III

'Twas Here, as old Traditions tell,
  A wither'd Witch was wont to dwell;
The magic Mutterings of whose Voice could call
A thousand Dæmons from their darksome Hall,
Bid haste the wild Winds from their Northern Caves,
Obscure the Moon, and rouse the roaring Waves:
Here *LUD*, retiring from fierce Battle came,
And from his Helmet quaff'd the cooling Stream;
Leant on his Spear, unrein'd his foamy Steed,
To pasture on the green, refreshful Mead.[16]

This is a poem which might have interested Collins, as well as Thomas Gray. The volume also contains a blank verse rendering of Moschus' Pastoral on the death of Bion which is by no means despicable as an English poem; a Spenserian imitation, "On the Death of Mr. William Levinz"; the two "Runic Odes" which, on the assumption that they probably influenced Gray, are about all of the elder Warton's poetry which is ordinarily remembered by anyone; and an "Ode on Taste" in that unrhymed lyric measure which Collins was to employ so triumphantly in "Ode to Evening." The collection shows the author to have been a man with an engaging range of interests, of considerable scholarship, and of an enthusiasm for literature which may have been infectious— which did infect his sons, and which may, through Joseph, have infected Collins. As I have said, we can never do more than strongly suggest an influence, yet I do want to do that.

In any case, and for whatever reason, Collins' powers developed with considerable rapidity while he was at Winchester. We have one poem from this period which we know to be by Collins, several others which are doubtful, and the *Persian Eclogues*. The first of the doubtful poems is verses "On Hercules" published in the *Gentleman's Magazine* for January, 1738. It is not a poem which on first sight one would claim or wish to claim for Collins, yet what claim there is for it is worth mentioning, and is based on a note in *The Crypt* for January 1, 1828: "The M.S. of the following Poem . . . was formerly in the possession of the great Thomas Warton, to whom it probably passed from his brother, the school-fellow and friend of Collins. In that family, we understand, it has always passed as a youthful production of the 'Cicestrian Bard'; it bears the appearance of a school exercise written out for the Master's inspection. . . ." [17] Although to me it bears no such appearance, it is certainly the sort of imitative satire a sixteen-year-old boy might have written. A joke about the cuckold's horns leading to a *double-entendre* on Hercules' club is certainly the sort of thing which a precocious sixteen-year-old could have thought enormously clever. Of its kind, it is not bad, as a matter of fact, and it is certainly a mode with which a young poet in the age of Pope would have had to experiment.

About the second doubtful poem there is to my mind less doubt. The "Song" (Young Damon of the vale is dead) was first printed with a note which surely seems to attribute it to Collins in the *Gentleman's Magazine* for February, 1788; it was first included among Collins' works in the 1790 edition of Johnson's *English Poets;* and it has generally been considered ever since to belong to Collins. The attribution has been challenged, but I still believe there is a strong probability that it is Collins' poem.[18] The editors of the Oxford edition of Collins, on what grounds I do not know, suggest that the poem was "perhaps written at Winchester in 1739," and perhaps, indeed, it was. Collins is here trying his hand at a bit of early "graveyard" poetry, and doing it with great delicacy and taste. The concluding stanza reminds one both of "Barbara Allen" and of Wordsworth—which in this case is not necessarily a recommendation. Yet, if the poem was really written in 1739 by a seventeen-year-old boy, that boy was remarkable both for his mastery of tone and for the way his poetic antennae were catching vibrations which would have been no more than barely audible at the time.

There are two other doubtful poems, "To Miss Aurelia C———r" and "Written on a Paper which contained a Piece of

Bride Cake," about which there is real doubt and which, if by Collins, do not in any case add either to his fame or to our understanding.

We can take more interest in the one very early poem which we can be certain is by Collins, the "Sonnet" (When *Phœbe* formed a wanton smile) published in the *Gentleman's Magazine* for October, 1739 (545). John Wooll in his biography of Joseph Warton provides proof for the attribution: "In a magazine," he writes, "I find the following memorandum, in Dr. Warton's Handwriting:— P545 Sappho's Advice was written by me, then at Winchester school; the next by Tomkyns; and the sonnet by Collins. *J. Warton.*"

"Sappho's Advice" consists of forty tetrameter couplets; nothing more need be said of it. The advice is that ". . . nymphs, regardless of their faces,/Should add *Minerva* to the *Graces*." "The next" is five ballad stanzas called "Beauty and Innocence" and, whoever Tomkyns was, they do not provide him with a very strong claim to be remembered. Wooll continues:

The three juvenile poets probably inspected each others compositions, and may be considered as jointly concerned in the pacquet sent to the magazine—A pacquet which called forth, from a critic by no means inaccurate or easily satisfied, the following unqualified eulogium:—"We pass on to three more of the lyric kind, which might do honor to any collection. There belongs to them an happy facility of versification, and the way to the scope of striking part is natural and well-conducted. . . . the least [the Sonnet], which is a favourite of mine, carries a force mixed with tenderness and an uncommon elevation." [19]

The eulogium, as a matter of fact, was simply a puff for the magazine published in the next issue and there is no reason to believe Wooll's coy hint that Johnson wrote it.[20]

As to the poem "When *Phœbe* . . .", it is interesting to consider John Middleton Murry's comments: "If at this point of time we are to be scrupulously just to Collins, we must recognize in his work a sensibility overweighted from the beginning by a precious literary instinct. The very perfection of the two schoolboy poems that have come down to us—'Young Damon . . .' and 'When Phoebe . . .'—is disturbing, for they show that the aesthetic impulse had reached the highest point of acuteness long before the sensibility could have established any real contact with experience at all. Those two poems are not excellent imitations; they are perfect achievements . . ." [21]

I shall return to Murry's arguments later. I agree that the perfection of "When *Phœbe* . . ." is disturbing. Collins had already mastered an idiom; the poem could fit without jarring into the works of a minor seventeenth-century "metaphysical." The poem is musical, allusive, dense in texture, intellectual. It is doubtful if that particular genre was capable of being pushed farther at the time, and these two stanzas, which already possess the very qualities which we will notice in Collins' greatest odes, must make us wonder where he was going next.

II *Oxford*

Physically, of course, Collins went next to Oxford; poetically, he went to the *Persian Eclogues*—something of a disappointment, but a perfectly explicable one. He was still experimenting, still searching for his own voice; and the *Eclogues* were a necessary part of that search. I shall return to discuss them in more detail in a later chapter, but now I must note that again Collins at a remarkably early age (though not so early, by a year, as Pope's achievement in the same line) has not only mastered a conventional genre but has also added something to it. It may have been, as Johnson would have said, a genre not worth mastering, but it was one which was publishable. And the publication of the *Persian Eclogues* in 1742, although anonymous, was Collins' first serious claim to public notice and, ironically, remained his chief claim to general fame during his lifetime. Joseph Warton said the *Eclogues* were written "when he [Collins] was about seventeen years old, at Winchester school," [22] but they were not published until Collins was at Oxford. We do not know, therefore, what alterations or enlargements the volume underwent between first composition and publication.

The publication of Collins' thin volume was no doubt a high point of his years at Oxford, but it perhaps did not compensate for what seems to have been an essentially disappointing experience. We must remember that the years at Winchester may have been a heady time for Collins: not only had the excitement of Classical and modern learning opened for an obviously alert mind, but he had also seen several of his poems in print and had composed the four longer *Eclogues*. In association with Joseph Warton he had become in a small way a literary personality and possibly the center of some attention. Joseph very likely led Collins in his early literary experiments, and, if this be true, he may have prepared Collins for some new and exciting ways of looking at the world through literature. Mr. H. O. White makes the point that "Collins was undoubtedly more than usually sensitive to the influences of literary friendship," [23] and, since boys in their teens are usually much less original than they think they are, it is hardly an injustice to Collins to point out relationships which may have changed his whole view of the world. Then, after he finished at Winchester, there was a severe disappointment even before the young poet actually entered the university.

Upon completing his studies at Winchester, Collins was admitted a Commoner of Queens College, Oxford, on March 21, 1740, and matriculated the next day, but he did not immediately leave Winchester. During that summer he was placed first upon the roll of students from Winchester to be received in succession at New College, with which Winchester had a special relation owing to their common foundation. Joseph Warton was second upon the roll, and John Mulso third. Had the election to New College actually taken place, it would have been a considerable boon both financially and, apparently, socially. Unluckily there was no vacancy at New College. "This," says Johnson, "was the original misfortune of his life"; it may have seemed so to young Collins at the time, and he may have communicated this feeling to Johnson later.

In retrospect, however, Collins would seem to have received some considerable palliation for his disappointment by his admission on July 29, 1741, as a Demy—or young scholar receiving half the stipend of a Fellow—of Magdalen College. His selection as a Demy was no doubt partly the result of the influence of his considerably older cousin, William Payne, a Fellow of the College. The Demyship seems to have carried less social prestige than the election to New College, but it made it financially easier for him to attend the University. The question of Collins' finances must occupy us later, but here I must point out that, if attendance had actually been financially impossible, it is not easy to understand why he had matriculated as a Commoner at Queens.[24]

In 1743 he took his Bachelor's degree, and in 1744 he resigned his Demyship (which he could have retained until he was twenty-five) and left the college, an action which seems to have astonished his friends at the time, but for which, I think, we need not search very deeply to discover at least a partial explanation. Collins the Winchester boy had promised a great career; Collins the Magdalen Demy was a disappointment. Langhorne, his first editor, remarks that

he was at once distinguished for genius and indolence; his exercises, when he could be prevailed upon to write, bearing the visible characteristics of both. This remiss and inattentive habit might probably arise, in some measure, from disappointment: he had, no doubt, indulged very high ideas of the academical mode of education, and when he found science within the fetters of logic and of Aristotle, it was no wonder if he abated of his diligence, to seek where the search was attended with artificial perplexities, and where, at last, the pursuer would grasp the shadow for the substance.[25]

It has never been clear where Langhorne got his information about Collins; however, we need only to remind ourselves of Gibbon's recollections of Magdalen College some ten years later:

To the university of Oxford [which he entered in 1752] I acknowledge no obligation; and she will as cheerfully renounce me for a son, as I am willing to disclaim her for a mother. I spent fourteen months at Magdalen College; they proved the fourteen months the most idle and unprofitable of my whole life: the reader will pronounce between the school and the scholar, but I cannot affect to believe that Nature had disqualified me for all literary pursuits. . . . In the discipline of a well-constituted academy, under the guidance of skilful and vigilant professors . . . I should have escaped the temptations of idleness, which finally precipitated my departure from Oxford. . . . The schools of Oxford and Cambridge were founded in the dark age of false and barbarous science; and they are still tainted with the vices of their origin. Their primitive discipline was adapted to the education of priests and monks; and the government still remains in the hands of the clergy, an order of men whose manners are remote from the present world, and whose eyes are dazzled by the light of philosophy. . . . The fellows or monks of my time were decent easy men, who supinely enjoyed the gifts of the founder; their days were filled by a series of uniform employments; the chapel and the hall, the coffee-house and the common room, till they retired, weary and well satisfied, to a long slumber. From the toil of reading, or thinking, or writing, they had absolved their conscience; and the first shoots of learning and ingenuity withered on the ground, without yielding any fruits to the owners or the public. As a gentleman commoner, I was admitted to the society of the fellows, and fondly expected that some questions of literature would be the amusing and instructive topics of their discourse. Their conversation stagnated in a round of college business, Tory politics, personal anecdotes, and private scandal: their dull and deep potations excused the brisk intemperance of youth. . . .[26]

Collins was clearly not one to satisfy himself with deep potations followed by long slumber. Gilbert White, then, hardly did justice to him when he wrote: "As he brought with him, for so the turn of his conversation discovered, too high an opinion of his school acquisitions, and a sovereign contempt for all academic studies and discipline, he never looked with any complacency on his situation in the university, but was always complaining of the dulness of a college life." [27] Collins, in effect, rebelled. His "rebellion," if that is not too strong a word, was not much different from that of many sensitive and intelligent college students today; in fact, it seems to have followed fairly typical lines if we may accept his ode "The Manners" as a comment on his own actions. This poem, as we now have it, could not have been written before 1745, but it pretty clearly constitutes a farewell to academic life:

> FAREWELL, for clearer Ken design'd,
> The dim-discover'd Tracts of Mind:
>
> .   .   .   .
>
> Farewell the Porch, whose Roof is seen,
> Arch'd with th' enlivening Olive's Green:
> Where *Science,* prank'd in tissued Vest,
> By *Reason, Pride,* and *Fancy* drest,
> Comes like a Bride so trim array'd,
> To wed with *Doubt* in *Plato's* Shade!

Youth of the quick uncheated Sight,
Thy Walks, *Observance,* more invite!

.   .   .   .

To me in Converse sweet impart,
To read in Man the native Heart,
To learn, where Science sure is found,
From Nature as she lives around:
And gazing oft her Mirror true,
By turns each shifting Image view!

.   .   .   .

O Nature boon, from whom proceed
Each forceful Thought, each prompted Deed;
If but from Thee I hope to feel,
On all my Heart imprint thy Seal!
Let some retreating Cynic find,
Those oft-turn'd Scrolls I leave behind,
The *Sports* and I this Hour agree,
To rove thy Scene-full World with Thee!
                              (1-2, 13-20, 25-30, 71-78)

In his "Second Eclogue" Collins had written, "Peace rules the
Day, where Reason rules the Mind," but a few years later it was
not reason but feeling that he sought. He was rebelling against
one cliché, not seeing that he was stumbling into another, and this
in a fashion very typical of a very young man who knows himself
to be a poet. Too much has been made of the supposed conflict
between reason and feeling in the mid-eighteenth century, and I
think that in their comments on Collins some critics have overem-
phasized this aspect of his rebellion.[28] Yet I see no reason to doubt
that a revolt against academe played an important part in Collins'
life in 1744-45. But we need not assume that such a revolt alone
prompted his turning away from the academic community to the
excitements of London. For one thing his mother died that summer, and her illness may have called him away, though it would
not have induced him to give up his Demyship. There are several
statements by Collins' acquaintances at first or second hand which
we can bring in evidence. John Ragsdale knew Collins in London,
or in Richmond, and in 1783 wrote a sketch about him to William
Hymers of Queens College, Oxford, who was preparing an edi-

tion, never completed, of Collins' poems. Ragsdale wrote of Collins' leaving Oxford:

Colonel Martyn [Collins' maternal uncle, of whom more will be said presently] greatly assisted the family, and supported Mr. William Collins at the university, where he stood for a fellowship, which, to his great mortification, he lost, and which was his reason for quitting that place, at least that was his pretext. But he had other reasons: he was in arrears to his bookseller, his tailor, and other tradesmen. But, I believe, a desire to partake of the dissipation and gaiety of London was his principal motive." [29]

Carver remarks, "Probably he [Ragsdale] did not know what a fellowship was, and may have confused it with the coveted scholarship at New College." [30] Ragsdale was writing long after the events; and, while we may depend upon his few circumstantial reports, we must disregard much of his hearsay—or invented—evidence. He was himself a tradesman, and hence noticed particularly Collins' debts. There is no other evidence for them, though we need not for that reason doubt Ragsdale. But debts to tradesmen were certainly nothing out of the ordinary in the life of an Oxford student, and hardly reason enough to leave the university.

Another story appears from the hand of an anonymous contributor to the *Gentleman's Magazine* for October, 1823:

. . . many a morning between chapel and breakfast have we lounged in its [Magdalen College's] *cloistered* walk, and turned back when we came to the naked trees; many a delightful hour have we passed among its hospitable members. . . . We have . . . eaten venison with contemporaries of Collins the Poet; and learned from them that he was a pock-fretted man, with small keen black eyes; associated very little; and was introduced into Magdalen by Dr. Payne, an uncle, whom he offended by refusing to pay attention to him, and therefore left the University.[31]

A quarrel with his cousin, a symptom of his deeper "rebellion," may well have been the cause that actually precipitated Collins' leaving Oxford, but I think there is still another consideration to bear in mind. In 1742 Collins had published the *Persian Eclogues*, and in 1743 the *Verses Humbly Address'd to Sir Thomas Hanmer*, "by a Gentleman of Oxford," both of which had a favorable reception. Hanmer had been Speaker of the House of Commons at the accession of George I and, though retired, was still a famous name. The occasion for the poem addressed to him was the publication of his pompous edition of Shakespeare, generally disapproved of by literary men but highly popular among politicians. Very possibly Collins hoped for his patronage, but there is no evidence that the hope was in any way fulfilled. Hanmer died in 1746. The poem went into a second edition in 1744, which in itself would have encouraged Collins to leave for London in that year to try his hand at the literary life. With the second edition, titled now *An Epistle: Addresst to Sir Thomas Hanmer* and considerably revised, appeared "A Song from Shakespeare's *Cymbeline*," Collins' most successful poem yet. The two poems were identifiable generally as his because for the first time Collins' name appeared on a title page. There was, then, some legitimate hope that he could successfully support himself by his pen.

III *London*

The hardships of the next few years in London have no doubt generally been sentimentally overstated. Mr. Carver, who goes into the evidence in exhaustive detail, convincingly demonstrates that the authors who have embroidered Johnson's hints of extreme poverty have considerably exaggerated. Johnson says only:

He now came to London a literary adventurer, with many projects in his head, and very little money in his pocket. He designed many works; but his great fault was irresolution; or the frequent calls of immediate necessity broke his schemes, and suffered him to pursue no settled purpose. A man doubtful of his dinner or trembling at a creditor, is not much disposed to abstracted meditation, or remote inquiries. . . . one day [I] was admitted to him when he was immured by a bailiff that was prowling in the street. On this occasion recourse was had to the booksellers, who, on the credit of a translation of Aristotle's Poeticks, which he engaged to write with a large commentary, advanced as much money as enabled him to escape into the country.[32]

Later on in the "Life" Johnson speaks of "a long continuance of poverty."

Johnson was acquainted with Collins, though how intimately it is difficult to judge. Certainly, in any case, his statements cannot be willfully disregarded; they are eye-witness evidence. Yet we must remember that Johnson was writing long after the events. When Collins was ill and in the care of his sister, Johnson mentions him with touching tenderness in letters to Thomas Warton; but we also know that, the more wretched the object of his attentions, the more profound was Johnson's empathy. Johnson had himself suffered the poverty which he attributes to Collins. Could it be that from the depths of his sympathy and in an effort to better understand a man, the essential springs of whose nature quite obviously eluded him, he is transferring to Collins some of the miseries he himself endured?

I mentioned that Collins' mother died during the summer he left Oxford. Her will, which for some reason was not proved until August 12, 1745, directed that the copyhold land within the Manor of Cackham, which she inherited from her husband, should be sold and the proceeds divided equally between her three children. The contents of this will must have been known to Collins in the autumn of 1744; he was, therefore, a young man with something more than mere expectations; he had a solid asset upon which he could receive credit if necessary. There is some indication, as a matter of fact, that he did ask for credit from another cousin, George Payne, a prosperous Londoner. What his immediate subsistence was in London we cannot say. Certainly he does not seem to have plunged at once into poverty, even though, as we shall see, there were no doubt some embarrassing moments.

Gilbert White reports, "In London I met him often, and remember he lodged in a little house with a Miss Bundy, at the corner of King's-square-court, Soho, now a warehouse, for a long time together." [33] It was some time between July and October that Collins found accommodations at Miss Bundy's, and to explain why he lodged in that particular house we need only remember his Winchester schoolfellow, John Mulso. Mulso's father owned a nearby house, and it was very likely Mulso who initiated the arrangement.

Ragsdale, nineteen years later, wrote that, when Collins came from the university, he called on his cousin Payne, gaily dresst, and with a feather in his hat; at which his relation expressed surprise, and told him his appearance was by no means that of a young man who had not a single guinea he could call his own. This gave him great offence; but remembering his sole dependence for subsistence was in the power of Mr. Payne, he concealed his resentment; yet could not refrain from speaking freely behind his back, and saying he thought him a d———d dull fellow; though, indeed, this was an epithet he was pleased to bestow on every one who did not think as he would have them. His frequent demands for a supply obliged Mr. Payne to tell him he must pursue some other line of life . . . This resource being stopped, forced him to set about some work, of which his History of the Revival of Learning was the first; and for which he printed proposals (one of which I have); and took the first subscription money from many of his particular friends.[34]

Although Ragsdale certainly didn't intend to do so, he presents a picture of a rather charming, if certainly irritating, young man just down from the university and quite full of himself. The account is probably substantially accurate. Very likely Collins asked Payne for credit against his mother's will (transactions in 1747 make this even more probable), and Payne, who was much older than his cousin, was reluctant to provide for a young man, of however good prospects, who had done anything so fantastic as to throw up an academic career and come to London with a feather in his hat to set up as an author. But Collins took his venture seriously. On July 18, 1744, John Mulso wrote to Gilbert White: "I saw Collins in Town, he is entirely an Author, & hardly speaks out of Rule: I hope his Subscriptions go on well in Oxford: He told me that poor Hargrave was quite abandon'd, that He frequented night Cellars; I am sure you will be sorry for it, it really concerns me when I think of it, that so sprightly a Genius & so much good-nature should be so thrown away." [35] From this we may doubt Ragsdale's implication that the history of the revival of learning was merely a bread-and-butter project. There is ample reason to believe, as we shall see, that Collins was deeply involved in it.

However, this scholarly interest did not provide immediate income. We have several indications of the manner in which Collins attempted to provide for himself. In the first place, Ragsdale says that "he engaged with Mr. Manby, a bookseller on Ludgate Hill, to furnish him with some *Lives for the Biographia Britannica,* which Manby was then publishing. He showed me some of the lives in embryo; but I do not recall that any of them came to perfection." The sequence of events is not entirely clear, but it may well be that these lives were the first of Collins' money-making efforts. The *Biographia Britannica,* a joint project of several booksellers, began publication in installments in 1745, and there may be unrecognized contributions by Collins in the first volume.

Another possibility for an immediate livelihood is revealed by a letter written by Collins' maternal uncle, Lieutenant-Colonel Edmund Martin (whom we have already briefly encountered in Ragsdale's sketch) from Fort William, Scotland, to the second Duke of Richmond. Colonel Martin had had the privilege of enjoying the hospitality at the ducal seat of Goodwood, near Chichester, and was on good enough terms with that nobleman to be an occasional correspondent and sometime dependent. He writes on September 17, 1744: "I am extreamly sorry my Nephew had ye Impudence to apply to You; I knew nothing of it, if I had he should not have done it; I never thought an Oxford Education was fit for anything but a Parson and they a Nuisance to ye Commonwealth." [36] This letter, taken with a tale reported by Alexander Hay in his *History of Chichester,* can explain a good bit about Collins' activities during the summer of 1744. Hay's account is confused and obviously in part wrong, but it leads us another step in tracing Collins' career. Hay tells the story thus:

In 1743 or 1744 he quitted the college; and at the desire of his mother's brother, lieutenant-colonel Martyn . . . went to Flanders, where the colonel then was; who would have provided for him in the army, but found him too indolent, even for the army; and besides, his mind was fixed on letters, and the improvement of his intellect. Returning, therefore, to England, he applied, by the colonel's desire, to Mr. Green, who gave him title to the curacy of Birdham, of which Mr. Green was rector, and letters of recommendation to the bishop, (doctor Mawson) then in London. With these, and the necessary credentials, he went to London; but did not go to the bishop's, being dissuaded from the clerical office by Mr. Hardham the tobacconist.[37]

[35]

Mr. Hardham, the tobacconist, intervenes quite abruptly in our narrative, and by his intervention played a decisive role in Collins' life. I shall return to him in a moment, but first there are a number of things we must sort out which are relevant both to Collins' life and to his poetry. We can see by Colonel Martin's letter that Hay was misinformed: the colonel was clearly not in Flanders at the time, and clearly did not desire that his nephew apply to anyone. As we shall see, Collins did, in fact, make two excursions to Flanders, but neither of them so early as 1744. I think we can suppose that what happened was something like this: Collins found that the public was not so enthusiastic about a history of the revival of learning as to flock to buy subscriptions, nor did his biographical writing produce much ready cash. His cousin Payne was not willing to trust him much further as a debtor. Knowing of his uncle's friendly relationship with the Duke of Richmond, who seems to have been roughly affable and was accounted by a contemporary as a "patron and admirer of The Fine Arts," [38] Collins applied to him for the assistance which, being patron of five clerical livings, he was certainly in a position to provide. The duke as a matter of course would have turned the matter over to his domestic chaplain, Richard Green, who informed Collins that there was a place for a curate at Birdham, of which he himself was rector. Collins returned to London in high spirits and confided his good fortune to John Hardham, tobacconist.

Why to a tobacconist? Hardham was a native of Chichester and for that reason alone might have taken some interest in his fellow townsman. However, he and Collins had other claims on one another's interest, for Hardham was an enthusiastic devotee of the theater and also the friend and employee of Garrick, for whom he counted the pit at a salary of 15s a week. Later on he was for a time under-treasurer of Drury Lane Theater. He himself wrote at least one (unsuccessful) play, and taught acting at the rear of his shop. The dates are obscure, but if Hardham was in 1744 already, as seems likely, established as a tobacconist, his shop must have been both a lively and interesting place, attractive to a lively and interested young man such as Collins, who might have met there not only aspiring actors but representatives of the fashionable world already arriving to buy the famous "No. 37" snuff upon which Hardham's fortune was built:

> A name is all—from Garrick's breath a puff
> Of praise gave immortality to snuff;
> Since when each connoisseur a transient heaven
> Finds in each pinch of Hardham's Thirty-seven.[39]

Garrick no doubt gave several puffs to Hardham's snuff, and perhaps introduced Sir Joshua Reynolds to this mixture to which he was so addicted. So when Collins returned to London with a curacy in his pocket, it was not unnatural that Hardham should soon know of it. Hardham was no doubt a shrewd man, and, if we can accept the dramatic swiftness implied by Hay's half sentence recording Collins' dissuasion, it must have been obvious to him that the young author was unsuited to a clerical life, but might be able to make his mark—and here he was sadly wrong—as a writer of tragedies.

Probably Collins' interest in the drama had already shown itself by the time of Hardham's exhortation, but it may have been Hardham who first directed his attention to the stage. Collins already knew Aristotle's dramatic theory; all that might have seemed necessary was to apply it. At any rate, Collins made some progress towards writing a tragedy, and certainly became known to the inner circle of the theatrical world. Ragsdale reports that, "He was an acceptable companion everywhere; and among the gentlemen who loved him for a genius, I may reckon . . . Messrs Quin, Garrick and Foote, who frequently took his opinion on their pieces before they were seen by the public. . . . From his knowledge of Garrick, he had the liberty of the scenes and green-room, where he made diverting observations on the vanity and false consequence of that class of people; and his manner of relating them to his particular friends was extremely entertaining." [40]

Probably it was in the early Autumn of 1744 that Collins began residence at Miss Bundy's. On October 8, Mulso writes to Gilbert White: "Collins is now my next neighbour. I breakfasted with him this morning, & Capn. Hargrave play'd on ye Harpsichord, which he has not forgott quite so much as He has Himself." [41] We can imagine that it was at Collins' urging that Captain Hargrave played the harpsichord, since Gilbert White informs us that Collins was passionately fond of music. There is certainly no indication from Mulso's letter that Collins was in any real difficulties, and I think we can gather from the tone of the correspondence that, had he been, Mulso would not have hesitated to mention it.

As a matter of fact, we are probably safe in assuming that the end of 1744 was a cheerful time for Collins. In A Literary Journal for the fourth quarter of that year, among notices of books forthcoming and already published appeared the following announcement: "The following books deserve also to be mentioned: . . . A Review of the Advancement of Learning from 1300 to 1521 by Wm. Collins. 4to." [42] The circumstances of this announcement remain extremely obscure. The title appears as one in a list of books which actually were published and had an actual physical existence. A Literary Journal was a private enterprise published in Dublin, and why Collins' volume was announced there, how the proprietor of the journal got his information, or to what stage the preparation of the book had proceeded we cannot guess; but we must suppose that Collins had made measurable progress. We know from remarks dropped by Thomas Warton that at some time in his life Collins had made a considerable collection of older literature, and this announcement gives us good reason to believe that these collections were already well established in 1744. There is, however, no mention anywhere of any tragedy by Collins on the way to completion. Indeed, the indications from the odes are that he would not have been a very successful dramatist; and, in an age when success as a writer for the theater demanded voluminous production, his meticulous habits of composition would have worked against him as a playwright—unfortunately, since the theater could provide financial success.

It has been traditional to read Collins' odes against a background of distressful poverty. I think such a reading does not much illuminate the poems and, as I have said, the evidences for such severe poverty as described many years after the events by Johnson and Gilbert White are not at all decisive. But this is not to say that Collins never felt a financial pinch. However involved the young author was in various literary projects during 1744, none of them had produced any profit, except possibly a few guineas for biographies; and we cannot even be sure that Collins completed any of these for Manby *et al.* But in early 1745 the prospects brightened considerably. On March 5, 1745, the will of Charles Collins, the poet's uncle, was proved, and this document bequeaths to "my Nephew William Collins son of Alderman William Collins . . . all my said freehold Estate with all Appurtenances belonging to it with all Rents Arrearages and Profits from it arising from one Year after my Decease to be accounted for to him." [43]

This inheritance has been a source of confusion among Collins' biographers, and it is worth pausing a moment to straighten out the situation. Mr. Carver, in an extensive search through official records, has discovered facts which enable us clearly to contradict the statement of Johnson that "Soon afterwards [Johnson leaves the precise time obscure, but he seems to have had 1746 in mind] his uncle, Mr. Martin, a lieutenant-colonel, left him about two thousand pounds; a sum which Collins could scarcely think exhaustible, and which he did not live to exhaust." [44]

Colonel Martin died in 1749, and there is no reason to think he had two thousand pounds to leave to his nephew or anyone else. Lord Albemarle, the Duke of Richmond's brother, wrote to the duke in 1746; "Martyn marched two Days ago to Perth, and from thence to Holland, your Letter has rejoiced the poor man, he is honest, brave, and means to do well, besides being careful, but his forehead is rough, besides being shaby in his dress . . ." Earlier General Hawley had written to Richmond, "As to your Friend Martin I cant helpe saying he is 'un pauvre sujet' in a Military way and he has certainly left all his good sense at Chichester, his covetiousness or his generosity are not at all points in question, his ignorance that has appeared in some things and his mean appearance I doubt he will have a hard task to get the better with the D[uke], I assure you I have nothing to say against the man but that he is beyonde his sphere and was surely intended by God Almighty, when made, to be only a Capt." [45] This report does not present a man who could leave anyone a third of a six-thousand-pound estate, or even a two-thousand-pound estate, in the mid-eighteenth century.

On the other hand, Collins' Uncle Charles clearly made his

nephew his principal heir, and appointed his "dearly beloved Nephews William Collins and Dr. George Payne" his executors. In addition to the property, Collins is to have his most treasured personal possessions, including,

> my Fathers Picture in a frame and my own picture without a Frame and Alexander taking Darius in his Court without a Frame and the Draught of Winchester College in a black Frame. Also I give my aforesaid Nephew William Collins my Silver Tankard with my Arms on it and my collection of Music on the Score [;] this collection of Church Music as well as songs and other Musick which if you have no relish of it now, it may be hereafter valuable therefore pray make much of it and keep it for the Love the Family have born to that Family.

George Payne inherits separate sums of forty pounds and thirty guineas, and Collins' sisters, Elizabeth and Anne, inherit one shilling each, and Elizabeth in addition inherits her grandmother's wedding ring.[46]

We observe, however, that the main provisions of the will did not take effect until a year after Charles Collins' death in early 1745. Mr. Carver reasonably speculates that Collins again had recourse to his cousin Payne. A prospective owner of one property in Chichester and part owner of another, Collins must have been considered a fairly good credit risk. It may be that Ragsdale refers to this period when he mentions Collins' calling on Payne, but it would surely have been a most natural thing to do either in 1744 or 1745. Now it may have been in early 1745 that Johnson "one day was admitted to him when he was immured by a bailiff" and recourse was had to the booksellers for the translation of Aristotle.[47] If Johnson's account is true, and there is no reason to doubt it, this must have been the time when Collins first went to Richmond and first met James Thomson. Ragsdale also lived in Richmond, and it is probably in the early months of 1745 that their relationship, whatever it was, began; and it is probably to the first half of 1745 that Ragsdale is referring when he writes:

> Both Dr. Johnson and Mr. Langhorne are mistaken when they say, the *Translation of Aristotle* was never begun: I know the contrary . . . from the freedom subsisting between us, we took the liberty of saying any thing to each other. I one day reproached him with idleness; when,

to convince me my censure was unjust, he showed me many sheets of his *Translation of Aristotle,* which he said had so fully employed himself about, as to prevent him calling on many of his friends so frequently as he used to do.

Ragsdale goes on to say that, "Soon after this he engaged with Mr. Manby . . . to furnish him with some *Lives for the Biographia Britannica,*" [48] but we have seen that this engagement was probably earlier; and if, as Ragsdale remembers, Collins was working on such lives, it was probably in fulfillment of the previous arrangement.

If this reconstruction is correct, we can assume that Collins spent several months working in Richmond, making, perhaps, occasional trips to London to visit friends (even Thomson often walked back and forth), but on the whole he was busily employed. It may be to this period, when Collins was concerned with Aristotle and perhaps still contemplating writing tragedies himself, that we can refer the inspiration for his first two odes, "To Pity," and "To Fear."

But this peaceful life did not continue long; for on July 25, 1745, the Young Pretender landed in Scotland, and the alarms of war sounded on British soil. It is hard to know what immediate effect this news might have had on Collins; that it had some effect we can easily guess from the four "patriotic" poems included in his volume of odes published the next year. He would not have heard of the war until the second week in August, [49] and perhaps like most of the public would not have been much concerned when he did hear; [50] but it may be, also, that he was one of the few who were alarmed, or it may be simply that he recognized a way out of financial embarrassment. At any rate the next we know of him definitely is from another of Mulso's letters, dated September 7, 1745: "—Collins has been some Time return'd from Flanders, in order to put on ye Gown as I hear, & get a chaplaincy in a Regiment. Don't laugh, indeed I don't on these occasions: This will be ye second acquaintance of mine who becomes ye Thing He most derides." [51] What Mulso means by "some Time" is hard to say; but, if it were no more than a week, and if Collins had been lucky in crossing the Channel, he could have made a quick trip to Flanders to see Colonel Martin and have already been in London again for "some Time" before Mulso wrote. There seems no reason to doubt that he went to Flanders to see his uncle, whose regiment was stationed there, and that his object in doing so was to offer himself for some kind of military service. His poem on the death of Colonel Ross and the ode "To Liberty" enable us, surely, to believe him capable of purely patriotic sentiments. And the fact that he was able to make the trip at all indicates no urgent financial strain, though we need not therefore believe that the small income from a military appointment was no consideration. This is probably the occasion, if any such occasion there was, reported by Hay when Colonel Martin found his nephew "too indolent, even for the army," and it may well be that, "Colonel Martin did not approve of him as a volunteer, even for the duration of the rebellion: but, remembering that the young man had once caused him some embarrassment by troubling the Duke of Richmond about an application for a curacy, he may well have suggested that it might be better to be incompetent in two professions than in one." [52]

Collins probably did not take his uncle's advice seriously; at least there is no further mention of a chaplaincy or a curacy, and when we hear of him again, again from Mulso, it is quite obvious that the idea of a clerical life has not much upset him. The letter is dated May 28, 1746:

I can't help telling You, tho' 'tis a little uncharitable, that Collins appears in good cloathes & a wretched carcass, at all ye gay Places, tho' it was with ye utmost Difficulty that He scrap'd together 5 pounds for Miss Bundy, at whose Suit He was arrested & whom by his own confession He never intended to pay. I don't beleive He will tell ye Story in Verse, tho' some circumstances of his taking would be burlesque enough. The Bailiff introduced himself with 4 Gentlemen who came to drink Tea, & who all together could raise but one Guinea. The ἀναγνώρισις (a word he is fond of) was quite striking, & ye catastrophe quite poetical and interesting. [53]

This poverty doesn't sound much like that Samuel Johnson described, but the report gives us a chance to reconstruct what may have been happening. After his return from Flanders, Collins managed to settle with the creditors who had driven him to the country the previous spring, though we needn't think he thereupon abandoned his visits. Indeed, there is reason to think his friendship with Thomson grew warmer. On April 10—no doubt as soon as possible under the terms of his uncle's will—he mortgaged the property in Chichester for fifty pounds, which accounts for his sudden appearance in good clothes at the fashionable places. On May 30 a William Milton paid the mortgage with interest due and purchased the freehold for an additional twelve pounds.[54] Even allowing for the difference in the value of money in the eighteenth century, sixty-two pounds was not enough to relieve a man entirely of financial worries; but, reckoning the pound in 1746 to have been worth about fifteen times its value today in purchasing power (it was probably nearer twenty), it is a considerable sum, though exhaustible.

By May, then, Collins has installed himself again at Miss Bundy's and, as a matter of fact, is in reasonably comfortable, if somewhat precarious circumstances. A good bit of his money has had to go to Cousin Payne in repayment of loans, but he has confidence enough to have bought good clothes and to be making an appearance as a young man of the town. However, Miss Bundy has had to wait for her rent; and, irritated by revelry in her tenant's rooms, she devised a catastrophe. There is no record of Collins' name in the prison books, so we can be sure Miss Bundy did not carry matters to the last degree. She was the daughter of a clergyman, and probably only wanted to teach her lodger an unforgettable lesson. The remark that Collins never intended to pay is surely one which Mulso heard from Miss Bundy, who had known the Mulso family for many years, rather than from Collins, who could hardly expect to evade so obvious a debt.[55]

The letter from Mulso also hints that Collins may have been still concerned with the translation of Aristotle, or perhaps studying Aristotle with a view to writing a tragedy of his own, for the unusual word ἀναγνώρισις can hardly have come from another source. It is a recollection of the *Poetics,* where it is defined (in Butcher's translation) as "a change from ignorance to knowledge, producing love or hate between the persons destined by the poet for good or bad fortune"—a singularly appropriate term for the surprise devised by Miss Bundy!

During the early months of 1746 Collins was working on his odes. They had probably been in progress for some time, but we are quite sure that by the summer of 1746 they were nearing the form in which we possess them. Probably it was in May, 1746, that he paid a visit to the Guildford races—one of the fashionable places at which he was now displaying his new clothes—and it was there that he met Joseph Warton. Together, in daring spirits, they came to the decision to publish their poems. The letter from Joseph to Thomas Warton gives no indication of date or place:

DEAR TOM, —You will wonder to see my name in an advertisement next week, so I thought I would apprise you of it. The case was this. Collins met me in Surrey, at Guildford races, when I wrote out for him my odes, and he likewise communicated some of his to me; and being both in very high spirits, we took courage, resolved to join our forces, and to publish them immediately. I flatter myself that I shall lose no honour by this publication, because I believe these odes, as they now stand, are infinitely the best things I ever wrote. You will see a very pretty one of Collins's, on the death of Colonel Ross before Tournay. It is addressed to a lady who was Ross's intimate acquaintance, and who, by the way, is Miss Bett Goddard. Collins is not to publish the odes unless he gets ten guineas for them. I returned from Milford last night, where I left Collins with my mother and sister, and he sets out to-day for London. . . .[56]

The mention of the ode on the death of Colonel Ross refers to its forthcoming publication in the June 7 number of Dodsley's *Museum;* it is, by the way, properly titled "Ode to a Lady. On the Death of Col. Charles Ross, in the Action at Fontenoy." A headnote says "Written May, 1745," but there are persuasive arguments for a later date.[57] We can only guess why the plan for joint publication fell through. Perhaps Collins could not get ten guineas; perhaps Dodsley, the bookseller who published Warton, with his shrewd intuition into popular taste, saw that Collins' poems would not strike the public fancy; perhaps—an invidious suggestion, but one which may help explain his later silence about Collins—Joseph Warton, on careful reading of Collins' poems, realized their great superiority to his own, and saw that he might indeed lose honor by joint publication. We have no way of knowing. The question is an intriguing one, and of some importance in the light of the short preface which Joseph wrote for his volume. I shall return to Warton's prefatory paragraph in a later chapter, but I should point out now that if we can legitimately associate Collins with it—as I think we can—it tends to confirm the hypothetical view of Collins as one of a conscious literary *avant-garde* of the 1740's.

We must keep in mind also, as a backdrop to Collins' life in late 1745 and early 1746, that Bonny Prince Charlie's abortive rebellion was still in progress, that in March the populace of London was alarmed by the advance of the rebel troops as far as Derby, and that on April 16 the Battle of Culloden finally ended Stuart hopes. These are events that are more than dimly reflected in Collins' poetry.

One of the things which pretty clearly is *not* reflected in his poetry, however, is a disappointed love affair with the Miss Bett Goddard mentioned in Joseph Warton's letter. Biographers have been trying for two hundred years to invent episodes of romantic love for Collins, but there is simply no evidence upon which to base such speculation. Bett Goddard was obviously someone known to Collins, the Wartons, and Ross. She is not known to twentieth-century scholarship. Ross, incidentally, was not a colonel, but a captain—which leads us to believe that Collins could not have been more than casually acquainted with him, and probably not much more intimately acquainted with his fiancée.

The early summer of 1746, then, Collins can be supposed to have spent polishing his odes with that special care commented upon both by Ragsdale and Thomas Warton. Was it as a relief from the intense concentration of this work that he made a second trip to Flanders? Our next definite date in his life comes again from Mulso in a letter to Gilbert White dated August 1, 1746: "I have just receiv'd a Letter from Collins, dated Antwerp. He gives me a very descriptive Journal of his Travells thro' Holland to that Place, which He is in Raptures about, & promises a more particular Account of: He was just setting out for ye Army, which He says are in a poor way, & He met many wounded and sick Countrymen as He travell'd from Helvoet-Sluys." [58]

Collins' biographers have commonly supposed that he went again to the Continent to ask his unfortunate uncle for money. As a matter of fact, his uncle's regiment did not begin marching from Scotland, where it had been sent as a consequence of the rebellion, until July 11; and on August 1, when Collins had already been traveling about for quite a while, it was still waiting for favorable tides at Burnt Island, Fifeshire. If Collins wanted money—and we have seen that it was in any case unlikely that Colonel Martin had much to spare—he was going the long way to get it; for, although he could certainly assume that his uncle's regiment would be returned to the war in Flanders, neither he nor his uncle could have been sure just where, or even precisely when. Moreover, it is hardly reasonable to suppose that, if Collins were seriously in need of money, he would decide to tour Holland. Nor does Mulso's report of the letter make it sound as though Collins were doing anything more than cheerfully exploring. The fact that he was "just setting out for ye Army" does not require us to assume even that he was going to see his uncle, whom he could easily have discovered was not yet in Flanders.[59]

Collins' odes were published in December. The *Gentleman's Magazine* for that month, among announcements of books published, "Entertainment and Poetry," lists

5. Odes on several descriptive and allegoric subjects. By *W. Collins* pr. 1s. *Millar*.

6. Odes on several subjects. By *Jos. Warton*, B.A. pr. 1s 6d. Dodsley.[60]

A similar notice appeared in the *British Magazine* for the same month. This was the high-water mark of Collins' life, although he could not realize it at the time; for Dodsley was right, on financial grounds, in deciding to publish Warton but not Collins. Warton's volume had a modest success; Collins' was virtually unnoticed.

We do not know what his reaction to this relative failure of his poems may have been. He can hardly have been very happy about it, and we are told that eventually he bought up the impression and burned it; but this, if true, was probably in 1749. We know that he was engaged in various literary projects in 1747, and one bit of hack writing from this period may be identifiable,[61] an essay titled "Of the Essential Excellencies in Poetry," published in *The Museum* for July 4, 1747 (281). It must be either by Collins or by someone mightily struck by the "Ode on the Poetical Character." The evidence for Collins' authorship is wholly internal, but it seems to me strong; moreover, the fact that we know Collins to have been published in *The Museum* the previous year makes the attribution even more likely. If Collins wrote this piece, it is at least possible that he wrote and was paid for others which we cannot now identify.

Some time during 1747 Collins and his two sisters disposed of the property on East Street, Chichester, left them under their mother's will and in accord with the terms of that document. One is only surprised that it had not been sold earlier, and the delay may indicate a pretty reluctance to let the property go out of the family.[62] More important to us is another document, the only manuscript in Collins' hand which still survives (except for a few annotations and signatures), a letter from him to John Gilbert Cooper. Cooper won a modest fame as poet, biographer of Socrates, and author of *Letters Concerning Taste* (1755), wherein he several times praises the "Ode to Evening." The letter shows Collins still to be cheerful, and is concerned with plans for a "Clarendon Review," which, Thomas Warton informs us, was to have been published under the aegis of the university. There is no evidence that the review was ever more than a plan—a sad fact, but explicable enough. "When it is remembered," as Professor W. C. Bronson said, "that the reviews of the eighteenth century were booksellers' organs, written by literary hacks, Collins's idea is seen to be original and bold. It has since been realized, in substance, by the great independent reviews established in the first quarter of the [nineteenth] century; in 1750 the project probably was not practicable." [63]

Many years later, Thomas Warton wrote:

I often saw Collins in London in 1750. This was before his illness. He then told me of his intended History of the Revival of Learning, and proposed a scheme of a review, to be called the Clarendon Review, and to be printed at the university press, under the conduct and authority of the university. About Easter, the next year, I was in London; when, being given over and supposed to be dying, he desired to see me, that he might take his last leave of me: but he grew better, and in the summer he sent me a letter on some private business, which I have now by me, dated Chichester, June 9, 1751, written in a fine hand, and without the least symptom of a disordered or debilitated understanding.[64]

We know from the letter to Cooper that the plan for the review was well advanced in 1747, and it is possible, then, that Warton may also be remembering that in that year Collins was again at work on the "Review of the Advancement of Learning," perhaps now under another name or in an expanded form. Certainly what small evidence we have shows Collins not to have been idle, and the letter clearly indicates that he was involved in the literary politics of the day. It is likely, too, that in 1747 Collins first met John Home, to whom he later addressed the "Ode on the Popular Superstitions of the Highlands," but definite dates in Collins' life become scarce after this time.

There is still evidence, however, that Collins remained active in literary circles. The depressing malady to which Thomas Warton refers in the letter quoted above clearly did not begin to afflict Collins until 1750 at the very earliest. In 1748 the writer of the preface to Dodsley's *Preceptor*—said by Boswell to have been Johnson—was very probably referring again to Collins' plans for Aristotle when he wrote ". . . a more accurate and Philosophical Account [of rhetoric and poetry] is expected from a Commentary upon *Aristotle's Art of Poetry,* with which the Literature of this Nation will be in a short time augmented." [65] 1748 was also the year in which Thomson died, so we may assume his visits to Richmond came to an end. Patrick Murdoch in his short "Life" of Thomson comments: "Only one gentleman, Mr. Collins, who had lived sometime at Richmond, but forsook it when Mr. Thomson died, wrote an ode to his memory. This, for the dirge-like melancholly it breathes, and the warmth of affection that seems to have dictated it, we shall subjoin to the present account." [66]

In 1748, also, Dodsley, perhaps allowing his critical to triumph over his financial acumen, included "Ode to Evening" and "Colonel Ross" in his *Collection of Poems . . . by Several Hands,* which kept those poems before the public in successive editions of the *Collection* for most of the century.

On April 26, 1749, Lieutenant Colonel Martin died, a fact that would hardly be worth mention except that, as we have seen, the poor man has deposited a cartload of red herrings across the path of Collins' biographers for two hundred years. There is no reason to think that Collins could have profited much, if at all, by his death, or that Martin would have had anything substantial to bequeath, except possibly what profit he might have made from the sale of his army commission. However, Collins did possibly enrich himself to some extent in 1749 by the sale (with his sisters) of the last of his father's property in Chichester. Technically, Collins disposed of his share of the property to his cousin George Payne (again in order to settle debts?). It could be, then, that to observers not intimate with his affairs, the death of his uncle was associated with some obvious accession of wealth, a part of which, according to Langhorne, Collins spent to buy up from Millar the remaining copies of the odes—an honorable and unnecessary thing to have done—which he burned.

Langhorne explains that, "Allegorical and abstracted poetry was above the taste of those times, as much, or more than it is of the present. It is in the lower walks, the plain and practical paths of the Muses only, that the generality of men can be entertained. The higher efforts of imagination are above their capacity; and it is no wonder therefore, if the odes descriptive and allegorical met with few admirers." [67] This is certainly true, but how much are we to make of Collins' reaction? Coleridge has said that, "There is a species of applause scarcely less genial to a poet, than the vernal warmth to the feathered songsters during their nest-building or incubation; a sympathy, an expressed hope, that is the open air in which the poet breathes, and without which the sense of power sinks back on itself, like a sigh heaved up from the tightened chest of a sick man." [68]

Collins had not been receiving very much popular applause for his poems, but whether he was receiving the kind of applause mentioned by Coleridge is not so clear. Dodsley had included him in an elegant collection; in June of 1749 the "Ode Occasion'd by the Death of Mr. Thomson" was published; and in October of the same year the *Gentleman's Magazine* printed the "Song from Shakespeare's *Cymbeline*," though anonymously and with an unauthorized textual change. I think it likely that buying the remainder of the odes from Millar was simply Collins' sense of fair play showing itself. After all, Millar must have lost money by the venture, and Collins' own youthful background was commercial, so he was performing what any honest tradesmen would have thought an obligation. The burning was no doubt in a fit of pique, but we have no reason to expect Collins to gaze at a shelf of his unsold works with the equanimity of a Thoreau.

On October 16, 1749, Collins and his sisters provided for the final disposal of their estate, and it was very likely on this trip to Chichester that Collins again met Home, in company with Thomas Barrow, the "cordial youth" of the first stanza of the "Ode on the Popular Superstitions of the Highlands," and shortly after that began composition of the poem.

There is good reason to think that another fertile creative period in Collins' life was beginning. The only fragment which remains is the "Superstitions" ode, a poem formally more complex than anything in the 1746 volume but the same time displaying a directness which few of the earlier poems possess. It is an intuition of greatness, and anyone who reads Collins carefully must lament that it is not in final form and that the other poems we know Collins to have composed about the same time do not survive. About only two of these do we have some definite information. One of them may actually have achieved publication and be awaiting discovery in some library or archive. In the *Whitehall Evening Post,* February 1-3, 1750, appeared the announcement that, "In a few Days will be publish'd, (Price One Shilling) An Epistle to the Editor of Fairfax his Translation of Tasso. By Mr. William Collins. Printed for R. Manby and H. S. Cox, on Ludgate-Hill." In the *General Advertiser* for Tuesday, March 27, 1750, was another announcement: "On Saturday next will be published, Price 1s., An Epistle to the Editor of Fairfax his Translation of Tasso's Jerusalem. By William Collins. Printed for R. Manby, and H. S. Cox, on Ludgate-Hill." [69]

Did the poem ever actually appear? Probably not, or it would have been discovered by now. But we cannot know for certain, and there is always the glimmering possibility that someone will yet discover it, bound in a volume, perhaps, with other poems published in quarto. Collins' fastidious demands for time to make more revisions may have caused the publishers to drop the poem entirely, of course. But we know the subject to be a very likely one for a poem by Collins, who mentions his interest in Fairfax in the letter to Cooper.

"No Common Loss"

Our knowledge of the other poem comes as a result of a performance in Oxford of a musical setting of Collins' "The Passions" by Dr. William Hayes, Professor of Music at the university, on July 2, 1750. Having been informed of this performance, Collins wrote Dr. Hayes (in the only other letter by Collins which has survived in any form):

SIR,—Mr. Blackstone of Winchester some time since informed me of the honour you had done me at Oxford last summer; for which I return you my sincere thanks. I have another more perfect copy of the ode; which, had I known your obliging design, I would have communicated to you. Inform me by a line, if you should think one of my better judgment acceptable. In such case I could send you one written on a nobler subject; and which, though I have been persuaded to bring it forth in London, I think more calculated for an audience in the university. The subject is *the Music of the Grecian Theatre;* in which I have, I hope naturally, introduced the various characters with which the chorus was concerned, as Œdipus, Medea, Electra, Orestes, etc. etc. The composition too is probably more correct, as I have chosen the ancient tragedies for my models and only copied the most affecting passages in them.

In the mean time, you would greatly oblige me by sending the score of the last. If you can get it written, I will readily answer the expense. If you send it with a copy or two of the ode (as printed at Oxford) to Mr. Clarke, at Winchester, he will forward it to me here. I am, sir,

With great respect,
Your obliged Humble servant,
WILLIAM COLLINS.

Chichester, Sussex, November 8, 1750.[70]

We can surmise that Collins wanted the score because a performance of Hayes' setting was planned at Winchester, and bibliographical evidence supports this supposition.[71] What is most intriguing, of course, is the ode on the music of the Grecian theater, which would have combined the great interests of Collins' artistic life in one composition which we could expect to be the most remarkable from his pen. But it is gone, leaving only ripples in a letter surviving by chance. Was the ode ever completed, or was Collins only searching for a pressure to make him complete it? Does a manuscript perhaps still survive behind some wallpaper in Oxford or in Chichester? And, if Collins wrote these two poems which are lost, how many more did he write which are lost and unrecorded?

IV *Chichester*

It must have been about the end of 1750 or in 1751 that Collins' illness began, and from this point on what little we can discover of his life is the story of his dissolution. We have already seen Warton declaring that at Easter of 1751 Collins was "given over and supposed to be dying," but recovered. This is the first datable evidence of disease, and, if we could only know the malady from which he suffered in the spring of 1751, it might provide the key to the mysteries of his later life. Johnson says,

He languished some years under that depression of mind which enchains the faculties without destroying them, and leaves the knowledge of right without the power of pursuing it. These clouds which he perceived gathering on his intellects, he endeavoured to disperse by travel, and passed into France; but found himself constrained to yield to his malady, and returned. He was for some time confined in a house of lunaticks, and afterwards retired to the care of his sister in Chichester, where death in 1756 came to his relief.[72]

Johnson's account is probably substantially accurate—except that Collins died in 1759, not 1756—and can be supplemented only in details. No one since the eighteenth century has added to our knowledge of this last period of Collins' life. Thomas Warton continues the letter previously quoted:

In 1754 he came to Oxford for change of air and amusement, where he stayed a month; I saw him frequently, but he was so weak and low, that he could not bear conversation. Once he walked from his lodgings, opposite Christ Church to Trinity college, but supported by his servant. The same year, in September, I and my brother visited him at Chichester, where he lived in the cathedral cloisters, with his sister. The first day he was in high spirits at intervals, but exerted himself so much that he could not see us the second.[73]

It was on the occasion of the visit to Oxford that Gilbert White saw Collins being dragged away to a madhouse. White accounts for Collins' illness by saying, "When poverty overtook him, poor man, he had too much sensibility of temper to bear with his misfortunes, and so fell into a most deplorable state of mind." [74]

Johnson diagnoses his case as "not alienation of mind, but general laxity and feebleness, a deficiency rather of his vital than intellectual powers. What he spoke wanted neither judgment nor spirit; but a few minutes exhausted him, so that he was forced to rest upon the couch, till a short cessation restored his powers, and he was again able to talk with his former vigour." [75] There is one final anecdote that indicates Collins may not have been insane in any accepted modern sense of the word. A Mr. Shenton, vicar of St. Andrew's at Chichester and the clergyman who buried Collins, reported to Thomas Warton: "Walking in my vicarial garden one Sunday evening, during Collins's last illness, I heard a female (the servant, I suppose) reading the Bible in his Chamber. Mr. Collins had been accustomed to rave much, and make great moanings; but while she was reading, or rather attempting to read, he was not only silent but attentive likewise, correcting her mistakes, which indeed were very frequent, through the whole of the twenty-seventh chapter of Genesis." [76]

Brydges says that "his shrieks sometimes resounded through the cathedral cloisters of Chichester till the horror of those who heard him was insupportable," though admitting that, "his reason, at times was sound." [77] But this statement was written eighty years after Collins' death, and probably based upon no authority other than the Reverend Mr. Shenton, whose anecdote contains the only contemporary account I can discover of his "raving." I would guess from the little evidence we have that Collins was intermittently in very great pain, from what cause we cannot now say, but occasionally of such excruciating severity as to cause him to cry out and act irrationally.

Among the few people to remember Collins in his last illness was Johnson, who in letters to Thomas Warton refers to him several times:

But how little can we venture to exult in any intellectual powers or literary attainments, when we consider the condition of poor Collins. I knew him a few years ago full of hopes and full of projects, versed in many languages, high in fancy, and strong in retention. This busy and forcible mind is now under the government of those who lately would not have been able to comprehend the least and most narrow of its designs. What do you hear of him? are there hopes of his recovery? or is he to pass the remainder of his life in misery and degradation? perhaps with complete consciousness of his calamity. [March 8, 1754]

Poor dear Collins! Let me know whether you think it would give him pleasure if I should write to him. I have often been near his state, and therefore have it in great commiseration. [December 24, 1754]

What becomes of poor dear Collins? I wrote him a letter which he never answered. I suppose writing is very troublesome to him. That man is no common loss. The moralists all talk of the uncertainty of fortune, and the transitoriness of beauty; but it is yet more dreadful to consider that the powers of the mind are equally liable to change, that understanding may make its appearance and depart, that it may blaze and expire. [April 15, 1756] [78]

So far as we know, Johnson had not seen Collins since 1750 or 1751, when Collins was last in London, though he may have seen him in 1754. It is hard to say, therefore, how much Johnson actually knew of Collins' state in 1756.

Collins died, according to the tablet in St. Andrews Church, Chichester, on June 12, 1759.

Such are the facts of Collins' life, connected by such speculations as I thought would do least violence to what we know. But from these facts the character of the man scarcely emerges. What was he like? What would it have been like to know him? He seems to have inspired affection in the people who knew him. Why?

The most perceptive and sensitive of the people who recorded their impressions was probably Samuel Johnson, and Collins was to Johnson clearly much of a puzzle. After remarking that "Mr. Collins was a man of extensive literature, and of vigorous faculties," and discussing with some implied disapproval the fictions upon which he exercised his mind, Johnson writes the following curious paragraph:

His morals were pure, and his opinions pious; in a long continuance of poverty, and long habits of dissipation, it cannot be expected that any character should be exactly uniform. There is a degree of want by which the freedom of agency is almost destroyed: and long association with fortuitous companions will at last relax the strictness of truth, and abate the fervour of sincerity. That this man, wise and virtuous as he was, passed always unentangled through the snares of life, it would be prejudice and temerity to affirm; but it may be said that at least he preserved the source of action unpolluted, that his principles were never shaken, that his distinctions of right and wrong were never confounded, and that his faults had nothing of malignity or design, but proceeded from some unexpected pressure, or casual temptation.[79]

Now what is Johnson telling us, or, more interestingly, what is he concealing? Who were the fortuitous companions? Captain Hargrave, who frequented "night cellars"? And was it in the night cellars that Collins kept the sources of action unpolluted, that he met the unexpected pressure and casual temptation? What were the "long habits of dissipation"? Gilbert White, in a passage I shall quote in a moment, mentions that Collins was "very temperate in his eating and drinking." What were the faults which Johnson seems almost to go out of his way not to mention?

When I come to discuss Collins' poetry I shall have occasion to point out more as a curiosity than as a significant circumstance the fact that so artistically passionate a man as Collins nowhere deals with sensual passion; that, for example, Love does not appear as a major figure in "The Passions," where by every expectation it would have a major place. Ensnared as we all are in the meshes of psychological speculation, we cannot help wondering if there is a connection somewhere between whatever it was Johnson was hinting at and the fact that Collins' poetry, with the exception of the doubtful and very early poem "On Hercules," is extraordinarily chaste, even cold. This sort of speculation, of course, is invidious and perhaps pointless, except in so far as it may help us to understand the poetry.

Gilbert White has left the following description:

He was passionately fond of music; good-natured and affable; warm in his friendships, and visionary in his pursuits; and, as long as I knew him, very temperate in his eating and drinking. He was of moderate stature, of a light and clear complexion, with grey eyes, so very weak at times as hardly to bear a candle in the room; and often raising within him apprehensions of blindness.

With an anecdote respecting him, while he was at Magdalen college, I shall close my letter. It happened one afternoon, at a tea visit, that several intelligent friends were assembled at his rooms to enjoy each other's conversation, when in comes a member of a certain college, as remarkable at that time for his brutal disposition, as for his good scholarship; who, though he met with a circle of the most peaceable people in the world, was determined to quarrel; and, though no man said a word, lifted up his foot and kicked the tea-table, and all its contents, to the other side of the room. Our poet, though of a warm temper, was so confounded at the unexpected downfall, and so astonished at the unmerited insult, that he took no notice of the aggressor, but getting up from his chair calmly, he began picking up the slices of bread and butter, and the fragments of his china, repeating very mildly,

Invenias etiam desjecti membra poetæ.[80]

"The poet remains, despite his scattered members." Johnson remembered the poet. The critic was not prepared to value the poetry, but he loved the man. Collins, "with whom I once delighted to converse, and whom I yet remember with tenderness," must have had rare qualities to evoke tenderness from Samuel Johnson. But what remains for us, of course, is not the poet, but the poetry.

CHAPTER 2

The Poetry and the Age

IF WE want to know Collins we must read his poetry—a simple enough prescription. Yet Collins' poetry is not, generally speaking, simple; and, if many people today find that eighteenth-century poetry sometimes leaves them blank, they may find that much of Collins' poetry leaves them blanker than most. A few of his poems—notably the "Ode to Evening"—are approachable on familiar terms, even though, as we shall see, those terms may need revision; but the bulk of his verse seems to most people to come out of nothing and to go nowhere, as foreign as though it had been written by Cynewulf or Caedmon. Readers today may react thus because Collins wrote bad poetry; on the other hand, they themselves may be failing in apprehension. I, naturally enough, accept the latter view, and in this chapter I shall try to show that some of the poetic techniques which the modern reader finds most alienating were the very ones which excited to admiration the contemporaries of Collins and Warton. That we do not respond to the same techniques is not necessarily our failure of taste, but rather the fault of an age, our own, which, like all ages, has set up certain absolute values for poetry which exclude more than they admit.

Thus the early eighteenth century seems to us just as perverse as we would seem to them in refusing to admit certain poems and poets to greatness. I would not be such a relativist as to suggest that, somehow, all poetry is good if we could only come to "appreciate" it. Most poetry, even of the great ages of poetry, is bad, bad by the standards of its own time and by ours. It is usually easy enough to find out what our own responses are; if we do not know exactly, there is always a critical journal to tell us. But it is not so easy to respond to poetry of the past with something of the vision of the past, to understand rather

than merely "appreciate," to bring to a reading of poetry an intellectual as well as a somatic response. In other words, it is not
easy for us in one age to pick out the good from the bad poetry
of another and to give some rationale for our choice.

That Collins wrote good poetry his own age came fairly soon to
agree. By 1770 his reputation was secure, though, as we have
seen, his poetry did not strike the taste of a quarter-century
earlier. Most students probably do not try to make what seems
the fairly fine distinction between the attitudes of 1745 and 1770,
yet it is necessary to do so. The literature of the eighteenth century is no more a monolith of heroic couplets extending between
Dryden and Wordsworth than American literature of the last
hundred years is a solid block of Emersonian marble, or English
literature between 1860 and 1960 merely a monument to Tennyson or Hardy. The shifts of poetic apprehension even within
twenty-five years can be considerable; and, in the period following the death of Pope, they were considerable. There are certain things we can say about the first half of the eighteenth century, perhaps more than we would feel safe in saying about the
first half of the twentieth; but we should be aware that for the
most part these are not the things the age said about itself, just
as two hundred years from now the first half of our century will
not appear to our descendants quite as it does to us.

These propositions are elementary, of course, yet I think they
have to be made. No one would think of reading Anglo-Saxon
poetry with the same eye he directs to Dylan Thomas, yet too
often we read mid-eighteenth-century poetry as though it ought
to have been written by followers of Wordsworth or Shelley. "But,"
you say, "Anglo-Saxon is really a different language." My point is
that, really, the poetry of Collins is written in a different language too.

I *The* kinds *for imitation*

As late as 1762 Allan Ramsay the Younger was able to produce
the following capsule history of English poetry:

. . . though none of our artists were inspired with the divine spirit
of Raphael and Corregio, our poets were much the worse for having
read Dante, Ariosto, and Petrarch; the imitation of whom they pre-

ferred to good sense and the imitation of nature. From this cause proceeded the tedious allegories, as they call them, of Spenser, and the jingling and strained conceits of Sir Philip Sidney. Happily for us there were no Italian models for tragedy; else Shakespeare's Othello might have been as poor as his sonnets. . . .

As liberty and order grew, learning and just sentiments flourished . . . The Royal Society was founded, and those hints which Sir Francis Bacon had given with regard to experimental philosophy were diligently prosecuted by the ingenious men of that age; so that authority began, by little and little, to give way to matter of fact, supposition to certainty, and words to things. But though in motion, still the progress of poetry was slow. It is not enough for poets to compose in times of good sense: it is necessary, in order to their writing well, that they should be born in such times. . . . Notwithstanding these new improvements in knowledge, the gentle Waller still decked his Sacharissa, with such unscented gum-flowers as had adorned the Laura of Petrarch; and still Milton thought it proper to march his angels in a cubic phalanx of well-bodied air, to attack as formidable a body of devils, who received them with cannon in their hands and puns in their mouths. . . . What greater instance can be required of the detestable influence of romantic and scholastic jargon, than its producing such a hodge-podge in the brain of a man who has given such proofs upon other occasions, of a truly natural and noble genius . . . [After the Revolution] metaphysics, now no longer necessary in support of opinions which were now no longer useful in the acquisition of power and riches, sunk by degrees into contempt; and Nature, having at last shown her true and beautiful face, poetry, from acting the part of a magic lanthorn teeming with monsters and chimeras, resumed her genuine province, like the camera obscura, of reflecting the things that are. . . .[1]

Ramsay was a successful painter, and in so far as he is a literary critic at all he is so minor as scarcely to exist; yet this very fact makes his capsule history interesting and relevant. He was no doubt reflecting a still respectable if very conservative literary opinion. To Joseph Warton and particularly, I should think, to Collins, these opinions probably sounded much as the opinions of the *Times Literary Supplement* may sound to Allen Ginsberg. As a matter of fact, Ramsay's opinions would probably have seemed extreme even to Pope. That he was able to express them at all helps to explain why Collins' poetry did not meet with immediate success. Ramsay was suffering from that critical myopia which afflicts most minor critics of every age: he was considering as true poetry only one, or at most a few, of several kinds of poetry. This was a distinction which the greater wits of the early century would not have failed to make, for the kinds of poetry were still seen as clear and distinct, and each kind aroused appropriate expectations on the part of the reader. The poet was, then, not so free to write as he chose as he is today; he had to learn a great deal before he could write "correctly"—write without offending the distinctions acknowledged by readers and writers alike. This situation, however stifling it might seem to poets today, was an advantage in that the poet did not have to create the taste by which he would be judged and by which he was enjoyed. Writing poetry was a much more communal affair than it has become since the early nineteenth century, and the possibilities for communication to a wide audience were consequently greater. The *kinds* of poetry were ready to be used; if a poet complied with the readers' expectations of the *kind* which he chose to write— that is, if he followed the "rules"—the product was accepted as a poem, good or bad, according to the poet's talent and material.

The reader will note that in writing I italicize the word *kind,* just as, were I speaking, I would give it that peculiar vocal intonation which indicates a word to be taken in a special sense. Indeed, it does have in my context a sense more precise and at the same time of more general import than we give the word when we say that "Dylan Thomas' is not the same kind of poetry as Robert Frost's." In saying this we recognize a difference between Frost and Thomas, yet we cannot specify that difference simply; for we will distinguish between Frost's lyric and narrative poems—and thus distinguish loosely what the eighteenth century meant by *kinds* of poetry—but when we speak thus of a *kind* of poetry, we do not make, as the eighteenth century did, a horizontal distinction, grouping individual works by various poets into a single large category. Rather, we tend to be more interested in distinguishing the characteristics of the work of a poet taken as a whole from those of the whole work of another poet. The early eighteenth century was less interested, for example, in speaking about the work of Alexander Pope and comparing it with that of Dryden (although Johnson, later on in the century, does just this, of course), than it was in speaking, to take one in-

stance, of Pope's satires and comparing them with those by Dryden or the Ancients.

The recognized *kinds* of poetry in the eighteenth century included the epic, verse tragedy, epistles heroic and familiar, the
epigram, the imitation (that is, a Classic poem adapted in matter
to the contemporary scene but retaining the spirit of the original
—a much-attempted but very difficult form), occasional verse,
georgic, pastoral, elegy, and Pindarick.* Translation was sometimes treated as though it were a *kind* of English poetry, and one
might make further distinctions by adding the prefix "mock" to
several of the *kinds,* or by subdividing several of them, but those
I mention sum up pretty well what an early eighteenth-century
reader would have thought of as poetry. In speaking of Collins,
we shall be concerned with only a few of these *kinds,* and particularly with the Pindarick; but we must not forget the background into which Collins' poetry fits.

Dominating a large space in that background is, of course,
Alexander Pope, who was acknowledged master in every poem
he essayed and who turned his hand to most of the acknowledged
kinds. He did not write an epic or a tragedy, though the translation of the *Iliad* counted for almost as much; and he was most
famous as a satirist in the epistle and mock-epic, or as a moralist
in the epistle and in imitations of Horace. Yet we must not forget
his recognized pre-eminence in the pastoral and in his one great
elegy, nor his considerable authority as a critic. By the time
of his death in 1744 he was the dominating figure in English
letters. To put it another way, he was a figure all set up to
be knocked down, for to say that he was a dominating figure is
not to say that everyone agreed with him; it is only to point
out that no one could quite get away from him.

It is too easy, however, to speak of the domination of a "School
of Pope," or to assume that such a school would have dictated
in this way or that. We need only to look at Thomson's success
eighteen years before Pope died to realize that Pope's poetry
was not the only sort which pleased. As a matter of fact, it is
dangerous to make assumptions as to what the effect of Pope's
dominance was, or would have been had he actually been a
literary dictator; for one need go no farther than the *Essay on*

* See p. 65 for explanation of this spelling.

Criticism (a piece written in extreme youth, when literary opinions are most apt to be inflexible) to find justification for almost everything Collins did. The fact is that, had Pope lived to see the publication of Collins' *Odes,* he would probably not have found so much to criticize as did Johnson later on, because Collins was adhering very closely to the concept of the *kinds* of poetry. He was writing in generally recognized forms and using them in an intense way which, had Collins or his friends done nothing to offend him, Pope might have been one of the first to appreciate. Johnson disapproved principally of Collins' idiom, on what grounds we shall see later—they were grounds quite intelligible and intelligent—but in critical viewpoint at large Johnson was sometimes uncomfortably close to his friend Allan Ramsay, perhaps closer to him, even at the time of the *Lives of the Poets,* than he was to Pope, or to Collins and Joseph Warton.

It is Joseph Warton who, in the "Advertisement" to his *Odes on Various Subjects,* 1746, is sometimes said to have produced the first document of the "Romantic revolt." To say this is silly. In so far as Warton—and Collins—were rebelling, it was a rebellion against the domination of a certain *kind* of poetry, not against the concept of *kinds* as such nor, as their poetry shows, against any of the essential precepts of neoclassicism. Since, as we have seen, there is some good reason to think that the "Advertisement" may reflect Collins' ideas as well as Joseph Warton's, it is worth looking at closely:

The Public has been so much accustom'd of late to didactic Poetry alone, and Essays on moral Subjects, that any work where the imagination is much indulged, will perhaps not be relished or regarded. The author therefore of these pieces is in some pain lest certain austere critics should think them too fanciful and descriptive. But as he is convinced that the fashion of moralizing in verse has been carried too far, and as he looks upon Invention and Imagination to be the chief faculties of a Poet, so he will be happy if the following Odes may be look'd upon as an attempt to bring back Poetry into its right channel.

It is, we notice, against the didactic poem, the moral essay, that Warton is "revolting"—against the dominance of a certain *kind* of poem. He could not have ended his first sentence as he did had he read very carefully the last book of the *Dunciad,* and his call for Invention and Imagination would hardly have startled Pope, who, after all, asks of the

> . . . bards triumphant! born in *happier Days*
> Oh may some Spark of *your* Cœlestial Fire
> The last, the meanest of your Sons inspire . . .
> [*Essay on Criticism*, 194-96]

and who meanwhile has spoken of the dull poets who

> . . . on the Leaves of ancient Authors prey,
> Nor Time nor Moths e'er spoil'd so much as they
> Some dryly plain, without Invention's Aid,
> Write dull *Receits* how Poems may be made.
> [*Ibid.*, 112-15]

What might have startled Pope in the poems themselves, and in the poems of Collins, was a change not in the primary concept of poetry—because I do not believe there was such a change —but in the models to which the young poets were looking; or rather, not so much in the poets chosen as models as in the poems chosen for imitation.

I think no one any longer is as astonished as William Lyon Phelps seems to have been sixty years ago to discover that Milton was read and imitated quite early in the eighteenth century. By the time Thomson published *Winter* in 1726, *Paradise Lost* provided as acceptable a model as the Classic poets, and critics were comparing Milton in sublimity with Homer. It is, indeed, bad Milton—that is, bad Miltonic blank verse—rather than bad Pope which is the scourge of anyone reading very deeply in eighteenth-century poetry. No one had yet lit on Milton's minor poems, which Thomas Warton the Elder and his sons tended for some time to think of as a sort of private preserve,[2] and it is the fact that the minor poems had not been rediscovered which may surprise us if we stop to remember that pastoral and elegy were among the accepted *kinds* of poetry. By 1730 or thereabouts, for whatever reason, Milton's minor poems had become models for minor poetry, supplementing, though not replacing, Horace, Juvenal, Virgil, and Dryden. Milton was being treated according to the best canons of neoclassic criticism as an "Ancient" upon whose example a modern poet could base his efforts.

It is hardly to be supposed, however, that the attention newly directed to Milton's minor poems constituted a very profound change in taste, though it may have constituted something of a change. The qualities which the Wartons, for example, admired in his verse were much the same, or thought to be much the same, as those to be found in another of the great and influential models for the shorter poems of the early eighteenth century, that is, the *Pastorals* and *Georgics* of Virgil. It is hard to overestimate the importance of this Virgilian minor verse to poetry in smaller forms written during the first half of the eighteenth century. If one becomes conscious of it, he finds the Virgilian influence almost everywhere. Dryden had made the great translation, and he spoke of the *Georgics* as "the best Poem of the best Poet." [3] Joseph Warton retranslated Virgil's smaller poems in 1753, and in his preface he speaks of the *Georgics* as "the highest flight of Virgil, and the master-pieces of his genius. . . . I think one may venture to affirm, that this poem contains more original unborrowed beauties and is more perfect in its kind as a Didactic, than the Æneid as an Epic Poem."

The basis for this admiration is not to be found in the subject matter of the *Georgics*, though that subject matter was itself often enough lamentably imitated in such eighteenth-century poems as Dyer's "Fleece" and Grainger's "Sugar-Cane"; rather, it was the Virgilian manner, the poetics of the poems, which elicited this praise. Warton speaks of "a profusion of the most daring metaphors and most glowing figures[;] there is a majesty and magnificence of diction throughout the Georgics, that notwithstanding the marvellous harmony and grandeur of the Greek versification, is scarcely excelled by Homer himself." In another place he speaks of the "transitions . . . [which are] the boldest and most daring imaginable, and hold very much of the enthusiasm of the ancient lyrics." [4] These were the qualities of verse associated in the minds of eighteenth-century poets, not with their own ostensible imitations of Georgic subject matter, but rather with another *kind* of poetry, the Pindarick ode.

II   *The Pindarick and the Sublime*

I shall not attempt to give a history of the Pindarick ode in the eighteenth century,[5] but I must make a few remarks about it as a form, for Collins called all of his greatest poems "Odes," and we need to find out what he had in mind when he did so. I must point out, incidentally, that I am not merely being whimsical when I spell the word "Pindarick" with a "k." By this spelling I mean to indicate the eighteenth-century conception of a particular *kind* of poetry, one which bore certain relationships to the works of Pindar, but which, soon after it was first popularized in the seventeenth century, came to have an independent life, very much as the modern circus may bear some fairly clear relationships to its Roman antecedents, though we seldom bother to think of them while watching a lion-tamer. The analogy is apter than may at first appear, for one of the characteristics which the eighteenth-century reader expected to find in the Pindarick ode, as Warton's mention of "bold transitions" indicates, was a disjointed kind of excitement. Other marks of the Pindarick ode were a dignified, perhaps "heroic" theme; a certain permitted irregularity, which was assumed to be enforced upon the poet by the tumult of his emotions (we must note, however, that metrical irregularity is not characteristic of Collins' or Gray's odes); and an extravagant daring in diction, phraseology, and metaphor.

As a recognized form, the Pindarick ode bears an interesting relationship to the extravagances of baroque architecture; and, just as there were many who disliked baroque architecture, there were many who disapproved of the ode. Addison we might expect to be one of these, and he does, to be sure, speak in the 405th *Spectator* of the "Absurdity and Confusion of Stile with such a Comparative Poverty of Imagination" in Pindar. However, Addison received his interesting rebuke from Collins' friend, John Gilbert Cooper, who pointed out that

Mr. ADDISON, was no *Great* Scholar; he was a very indifferent Critic, and a worse Poet; yet from the happy Mixture, just mentioned, he was blessed with a Taste truly delicate and refined. This rendered him capable of distinguishing *what were* Beauties in the Works of others, tho' he could not account so well *why they were so*, for want of that deep Philosophical Spirit which is requisite in Works of Criticism. He

likewise translated the Poetical Descriptions of OVID very elegantly
and faithfully in his own Language, tho' he fell infinitely short of them
in his own original Compositions, for want of that *unconstrained* Fire
of Imagination, which constitutes the true Poet.[6]

Note the last sentence. "Unconstrained fire of imagination" was
exactly the quality which the writer of Pindaricks was particularly
supposed to have. Cooper, like Ramsay, is limiting his conception
of the poet to one who produces certain *kinds* of poetry. Nobody
would have expected, I think, so much fiery imagination in a
moral epistle.

We can see something of the actual workings of the Pindarick
in Dyer's "Grongar Hill" Most of us are familiar with the poem in
its revised form as it appeared in David Lewis' *Miscellaneous Poems* in 1726:

> *Silent Nymph,* with curious Eye!
> Who, the purple Ev'ning, lye
> On the Mountain's lonely Van,
> Beyond the Noise of busy Man,
> Painting fair the form of Things,
> While the yellow Linnet Sings
> Come with all thy various Hues,
> Come, and thy Sister Muse;
> Now while *Phœbus* riding high
> Gives Lustre to the Land and Sky!

This could be, as we shall see, a mild sort of "ode," though not
Pindarick. It is Miltonic after the manner of "L'Allegro" and it is
interesting to compare it with another version, published also in
1726 as a Pindarick in Richard Savage's *Miscellaneous Poems and
Translations* (p. 60):

> *Fancy!* Nymph that loves to lye
> On the lonely Eminence;
> Darting Notice thro' the Eye,
> Forming Thought, and feasting Sense:
> Thou! that must lend Imagination Wings,
> And stamp Distinction, in all Worldly Things!
> Come, and with thy various *Hues,*
> Paint and adorn thy *Sister* Muse

> Now, while the Sun's hot Coursers, bounding high;
> Shake Lustre on the Earth, and burn, along the Sky.

As a matter of fact, Dyer is not able to sustain this pseudo-rapture much beyond the lines quoted, but it is easy to see from these quotations what the effect of the Pindarick was supposed to be on a poetic idea. In the hands of a Dyer, it was a dangerous effect; it was one which, between Dryden and Keats, only Collins and Gray were able to carry off. What Dyer tried feebly to do in the Pindarick version was to simulate an unconstrained fire, a wildness of imagination, a breathless ecstasy considered appropriate to the *kind* of poetry he was attempting. The Pindarick was not, then, primarily a matter of metre or stanza form; after Congreve's essay in 1706, the odes were frequently perfectly "regular," that is, followed strictly the pattern of strophe, antistrophe, and epode. The essential thing in the Pindarick ode was a rapturous effusion of genius, a genius distinguished, as William Duff said, ". . . by a WILDNESS of Imagination. . . . This character is formed by an arbitrary assemblage of the most extravagant, uncommon, and romantic ideas, united in the most fanciful combinations; and is displayed in grotesque figures, in surprising sentiments, in picturesque and inchanting description." This is almost a description of the Pindarick ode. Duff goes on:

A glowing order of Imagination is indeed . . . the very soul of Poetry. It is the principal source of INSPIRATION; and the Poet who is possessed of it, like the *Delphian* Priestess, is animated with a kind of DIVINE FURY. The intenseness and vigour of his sensations produce that ENTHUSIASM of Imagination, which as it were hurries the mind out of itself; and which is vented in warm and vehement description, exciting in every susceptible breast the same emotions that were felt by the Author himself. It is this ENTHUSIASM which gives life and strength to poetical representations, renders them striking imitations of nature, and thereby produces that inchanting delight which genuine Poetry is calculated to inspire.[7]

Now we do not have to read very far in the poetry of the first half of the century before we realize that, while remarks such as Duff's may provide criteria to be followed in the judgment of a poem, they are not very often regarded as precepts to be followed in its composition. Most of the poetry is certainly not very "wild" in the way the contemporary authors might have interpreted the term, and in this connection we must remind ourselves that no matter how the age defined genius, one of the ways it continued to define literature was in terms of imitating nature (as we see even in Duff) and particularly in terms of "correctness." The tension between "wildness" and "correctness" was not often resolved successfully; we shall see later how Collins attempted to reconcile them.

But this pursuit of "wildness" was not merely a vulgar display of the poet's genius. He was, by the consent of his readers, attempting to achieve something. Most often he was trying to scale the heights of poetic inspiration in order to reach the "sublime." According to eighteenth-century writers on the subject, obscurity was one of the attributes of sublimity; perhaps it is for this reason that the concept of sublimity itself remains somewhat obscure.[8] In so far as we need to involve ourselves in this tortuous subject as an approach to the poetry of Collins, it may be enough to quote from James Beattie's "Illustrations on Sublimity" in which, following Longinus at a distance, he set up two marks of the sublime:

Poetry is sublime, when it elevates the mind. . . . I speak here of sentiments so happily conceived and expressed, as to raise our affections above the low pursuits of sensuality and avarice, and animate us with the love of virtue and of honour. . . .

Poetry is sublime, when it conveys a lively idea of any grand appearance in art or nature. . . . [Virgil's description] in the first book of the Georgick, of a dark night, with wind, rain, and lightening: when Jupiter appears, encompassed with clouds and storms. . . . But in the style of a dreadful magnificence, nothing is superior, and scarce any thing equal, to Milton's representation of hell and chaos, in the first and second books of Paradise Lost.[9]

There was a great deal of writing about "the sublime" in the mid-eighteenth century, and the passage I have quoted hardly hints at the complexity which even the age itself saw in the subject. The creation or evocation of sublimity in a work of art was the farthest reach of human genius, and the most eminent critics of the time felt obliged to discuss the matter. We can see from Beattie's remarks that the sublime in poetry was double-barrelled:

it was both rhetorical—in that there was an emphasis on the conception and expression of great thoughts—and also plastic, in that great objects, objects of which all men stand in awe, such as gods, demons, hell, miracles, thunder, inundations, tempests, are to be so powerfully evoked that the reader feels himself in their presence. When Collins writes in "Ode to Fear"

> *Danger,* whose Limbs of Giant Mold
> What mortal Eye can fix'd behold?
> Who stalks his Round, an hideous Form,
> Howling amidst the Midnight Storm,
> Or throws him on the ridgy Steep
> Of some loose hanging Rock to sleep:
> And with him thousand Phantoms join'd,
> Who prompt to Deeds accurs'd the Mind . . .   (10-17)

he is being sublime, as he is also in the antistrophe of the "Ode to Liberty":

> Beyond the Measure vast of Thought,
> The Works, the Wizzard *Time* has wrought!
>   The *Gaul,* 'tis held of antique Story,
> Saw *Britain* link'd to his now adverse Strand,
>   No Sea between, nor Cliff sublime and hoary,
> He pass'd with unwet Feet thro' all our Land.
>   To the blown *Baltic* then, they say,
>   The wild Waves found another way,
> Where *Orcas* howls, his wolfish Mountains rounding;
>   Till all the banded West at once 'gan rise,
> A wide wild Storm ev'n Nature's self confounding,
>   With'ring her Giant Sons with strange uncouth
>   Surprise.   (64-75)

   In the first quotation our minds are clearly being elevated above the "low pursuits of sensuality and avarice" by being forced to consider a more elevated topic, the abstract notion of Danger; and the ode as a whole is intended to interest us in the "sublime" idea—that is, the idea animating us with the love of honor—*fear.* The poem is more complicated than that, but what I have said suffices to point out the "sublime" intentions. We also have in both quotations the effort to convey a lively idea of a grand appearance in nature—storms, cliffs, the agitated sea. And there is in both something "Beyond the Measure vast of Thought," something frightening, taking us out of ourselves because of hints of a tremendous obscurity which just in itself would have told the mid-eighteenth-century reader that he was expected to recognize something sublime. That these readers responded to this sort of thing is evident from the number of Pindarick odes attempted and, a few years later, by the esteem many readers were coming to feel for Collins' poems. Even Wordsworth at the end of the century had the same expectations, as we can see when he wrote of "Tintern Abbey": "I have not ventured to call this Poem an Ode; but it was written with a hope that in the Transitions, and the impassioned music of the versification, would be found the principal requisites of that species of composition." [10] That we do not respond in the same way is only to be expected, just as we need not expect readers in the twenty-second century to respond quite as some of us do either to T. S. Eliot's patient etherized upon a table or to Mr. Ginsberg's *Howlings*.

Not everything called an "ode" was Pindarick; but, when we get beyond the Pindarick mode, definition becomes perilous. It appears that any short poem could be called an ode; there is otherwise no discernible reason why Collins should have given "How Sleep the Brave" that denomination. Generally, however, as in "Ode to Evening," the verses are addressed *to* someone or something, whether or not in the bated breaths of the Pindarick style. The Pindarick was always intended to touch the sublime; and, when a poet announced his poem explicitly or implicitly as being in that mode, the reader knew what to expect. An "ode," without the earmarks of the Pindarick, might be almost any short poem, generally on a serious subject, and generally vocative.

III *Prosopopoeia*

The first of the two quotations from Collins' odes brings us to the discussion of another attribute of eighteenth-century poetry, and particularly of Collins' poetry, which at least puzzles the modern reader and may quite alienate him. *Danger,* we will remember, is not just an emotion; he is an active figure hideously stalking and howling. He is a personified abstraction. The question of these personifications is one with which we must particu-

larly concern ourselves since they appear in virtually all of Collins'
poems and constitute one of the hallmarks of his style. They are as
essential in Collins' rhetoric as the balanced sentence is in Samuel
Johnson's, and they are considerably more difficult for the twentieth-century reader to accustom himself to; for conscious personification is scarcely a part of our literary language, while it was a
very important part of the language in which Collins and his contemporaries thought.

I cannot concern myself here in detail with the whole subject,
though the reader who is seriously interested in eighteenth-
century poetry will have to do so.[11] However, since to bring to a
reading of Collins' poetry the usual twentieth-century attitude toward personified abstractions is virtually to destroy the poetry, I
must make some observations which may lead the willing reader
a little further into the universe of Collins' discourse.

Collins entitled his volume *Odes on Several Descriptive and
Allegoric Subjects.* The title is inaccurate from the point of view
of a post-Romantic reader, for most of us today would consider
only the "Ode to Evening" at all descriptive, and that not descriptive in the Wordsworthian sense we automatically attach to the
word. And, if we are precise in our literary terminology, we would
have to complain that none of the poems were, strictly speaking,
allegorical. There are the personified Pity, Fear, Simplicity, and so
on; but they do not *do* anything to make an allegory. We might
object that Collins' title says it is the *subjects* not the *poems* which
are descriptive and allegoric, but I do not see that such grammati-
cal precision helps. A descriptive or allegoric subject would seem
to demand description and allegory in the poem written on that
subject. Clearly, the words meant something to Collins and to his
contemporaries which they do not mean to us, and the word "allegory" probably did not mean to Collins quite what it meant to
Addison when he wrote in the 501st *Spectator:* "As some of the
finest Compositions among the Ancients are in Allegory, I have
endeavoured in several of my Papers, to revive that Way of Writing, and I hope I have not been altogether unsuccessful in it: For
I find there is always a great Demand for those particular Papers. . . ."

Addison was referring to allegory as a story in which, like the
Faerie Queene, the personified abstractions are given a part to

play in order to impress upon the reader the particular moral qualities they personify. The fact that everybody likes a story no doubt improved Addison's sales. In a sense *Danger,* in the passage quoted from "Ode to Fear," may also be playing a part, yet we would not call this an allegorical passage because there is no narrative. Actually most of Collins' personifications, and most of those of his contemporaries, are static rather than active; and they were clearly intended to be so. Collins never makes an effort to write what dictionaries of literary terms call an allegory. The "allegoric subject," then, is not an allegory, but rather a character which might be put into an allegory; in other words, a personification or prosopopoeia. "Fear" is an "allegoric subject" and also a descriptive subject, because, as personified, it describes—literally "writes down"—the emotion for us to see and vicariously to experience.

It seems incredible to us in the post-Wordsworthian age, but the eighteenth-century reader found this a particularly powerful and vivid means of expression. John Ogilvie writes, in 1762, of a "certain picturesque vivacity of description" as characteristic of the ode: "In this we permit the Lyric Poet to indulge himself with greater freedom than any other, because beauties of this kind are necessary to the end of exciting admiration. It is the peculiar province of imagination to give that life and expression to the ideas of the mind, by which Nature is most happily and judiciously imitated. By the help of this poetical magic the coldest sentiments become interesting, and the most common occurrences arrest our attention."

Ogilvie also explains the anomaly we noted above with regard to the term "allegory": "It is obvious, that in Lyric Poetry the Author cannot run into this series of methodised allegory, because the subjects of the Ode are real incidents which would be disfigured by the continued action of fictitious personages. His descriptions, therefore, ought to be concise, diversified, and adapted properly to that train of sentiment which he is employed to illustrate. When this is the case, we are highly entertained with frequent personifications, as these are criterions by which we estimate the genius of the Poet."

Ogilvie then discusses personification in more detail:

[72]

When an intellectual idea falls under the cognizance of an external sense, it is immediately surveyed with an accuracy proportioned to its importance, and to the distance at which we suppose it to be placed. We judge of Virtue and Vice, when represented as persons, in the same manner as we judge of men whose appearance is suggested by memory; and we therefore expect that these ideal figures shall be discriminated from each other by their dress, attitudes, features, and behaviour. . . . Nay, odd as it may appear, it is yet certain, that in many instances our idea of the imaginary person may be more distinct and particular than that of the real one . . . our ideas of imaginary persons are generally so exact, that upon seeing a group of these displayed on a plate, we are capable to give each its proper designation, as soon as we observe it. Thus Anger, Revenge, Despair, Hope &c. can be distinguished from each other almost as easily when they are copied by the pencil, as when *we feel their influence on our own minds, or make others observe it on our actions.*

From this detail it obviously follows, that as our ideas of imaginary personages are more just and accurate, than those which are excited merely by a particular relation of the actions of real ones; so we will judge with more certainty of the precise colouring which belongs to the former, and of the propriety with which they are introduced, than we can possibly do with regard to the latter.[12]

I must apologize for inserting so long a quotation, but it is likely that, without more substantive proof than my word, a twentieth-century reader will simply not believe that his counterparts of two hundred years ago reacted as Ogilvie and others obviously did. From Ogilvie's remarks we can deduce that the eighteenth-century reader was required to expend not necessarily more imaginative energy while reading a poem than we are accustomed to do today, but an imaginative energy of quite a different order. We would make a statement precisely the reverse of that in the last-quoted sentence by Ogilvie; poets and readers now find "just and accurate" only the ideas aroused by a particular relation of the actions of real persons, and we would say that our ideas of imaginary personages—personifications—are vague and insubstantial, hence unpoetic. Ogilvie was by no means eccentric in his opinions. Joseph Warton—whom I would like to quote on the probability that he and Collins had exchanged critical shop-talk—remarks:

It is the peculiar privilege of poetry, not only to place material objects in the most amiable attitudes, and to clothe them in the most graceful dress, but also to give life and motion to immaterial beings; and form, and colour, and action, even to abstract ideas; to embody the virtues, the vices, and the passions; and to bring before our eyes, as on a stage, every faculty of the human mind.

Prosopopoeia, therefore, or personification, conducted with dignity and propriety, may be justly esteemed one of the greatest efforts of the creative power of a warm and lively imagination.[13]

One of the praises which Warton bestows on Virgil's *Georgics* is that "We may justly apply to him what Aristotle thought so high commendation of Homer, that he found out LIVING WORDS. . . . To use Aristotle's expression, *Every thing in this poem hath Manners,* and all creation is animated." [14]

With these examples before us, we are tempted to believe that there really is a fundamental difference in the way our minds work now compared to the way people thought in the pre-Romantic age; and the fact that the method of prosopopoeia was actually used as a technique of exposition in a way which would be quite unthinkable today tends to confirm that impression. Consider, for example, an entry in the table of contents for John Gilbert Cooper's *Letters on Taste:*

"Letter XX. A mythological Genealogy *of* TASTE. CONTEMPLA-TION *was the Daughter of* JUPITER, (*who sprung from his Brain, like* PALLAS) *by whom* APOLLO *had a Son named* EUDOXUS [*i.e. true* KNOWLEDGE] *who beget* CALOCAGATHIA, *or* TASTE, *on one of the* GRACES." [15]

Even the twentieth-century reader stopping to ponder this mythological genealogy for a moment may be aware of having come to understand something of Cooper's idea of taste—conveyed perhaps more effectively than in straightforward exposition (How, exactly, would one convey the overtones of Cooper's idea in straightforward exposition?)—and this, of course, is what it was intended to do. The generalized abstractions of the eighteenth century are, we must remember, means not merely of decoration but of communication. That we are no longer able effectively to communicate in this way must be our loss, since it reduces our range, and reflects, therefore, not on the eighteenth century but on our own inability to arrive at the secure generalizations which such personifications represent.[16] The poet today does not regard an experience as valid until he has related it to a personal reaction—to his viscera, we are tempted to say unkindly; the neoclassic poet could regard an experience worth setting down only after he had put it in relation to a universal idea. It was the universal idea which men found most moving because it was in this realm that man's *truest* experiences lay.

It was because the habit of generalizing in personifications was so much a part of men's thinking in the mid-eighteenth-century that the highest reaches of personification were ordinarily associated with the "sublime." Robert Dodsley, discussing rhetoric in *The Preceptor,* says of personification:

There is an excess of *Passion,* a Degree of *Euthusiasm* in this sublime *Figure;* and therefore 'tis dangerous and ridiculous to use it, but when the Importance and Grandeur of the Subject requires such a noble Vehemence. . . .

This Figure animates all Nature; gratifies the Curiosity of Mankind with a constant Series and Succession of Wonders; raises and creates new Worlds and Ranks of rational Creatures, to be Monuments of the *Poet's* Wit, to espouse his *Cause* and speak his *Passion.* . . .[17]

And Henry Pemberton, discussing metaphor, speaks of that form of metaphor "when actions of life and sense are ascribed to inanimate beings. This last Quintilian observes to be the boldest, and also the sublimest form of this figure."[18] One of his examples, chosen from Richard Glover's *Leonidas,* reminds us of Collins' personification of Danger (We should note, by the way, that personification has nothing whatsoever to do with the capitalization of abstract nouns. Capitalization was a printer's convention, not an author's.):

> Before him terror strides, gigantic death
> And desolation at his side attend
> With all the furies of insatiate war.
> [*Leonidas,* IX, 48]

Joseph Spence speaks of "The *animating* Metaphor, tho' the most Sublime, and most Daring of any . . . I am pleased to see, that

Figure stands on such good reason; for it is the very life and Soul of Description." [19] Perhaps the most clearly worked out rationale for personification comes from David Hume. The process of abstracting itself first engages him in an effort to find out from whence our idea of God arises: "The mind rises gradually, from inferior to superior: By abstracting from what is imperfect, it forms an idea of perfection." Later on he expounds more specifically how the eighteenth-century mind produced poetic personifications:

There is an universal tendency amongst mankind to conceive all beings like themselves, and to transfer to every object those qualities, with which they are familiarly acquainted, and of which they are intimately conscious. We find human faces in the moon, armies in the clouds; and by a natural propensity, if not corrected by experience and reflection, ascribe malice and good-will to every thing that hurts or pleases us. Hence the frequence of the *prosopopoeia* in poetry, where trees, mountains and streams are personified, and the inanimate parts of nature acquire sentiment and passion. And tho' these poetical figures and fictions gain not on the belief, they may serve, at least, to prove a certain tendency in the imagination, without which they could neither be beautiful nor natural.[20]

Whether that "certain tendency" exists in the imaginations of persons today and is suppressed only by custom might be an interesting point to consider, but that it did exist in the imaginations of the mid-eighteenth century there should by now be no doubt. Mr. Wasserman points out the extent to which this tendency resulted from the education of the time with its emphasis upon certain Classical allegorists and Classical and Renaissance rhetoric;[21] but, whatever the reason for its frequent use, literary personification was not dryly academic but a natural language of spontaneity and passion. How natural a language it was conceived to be may be seen from Duff:

ORIGINAL GENIUS will naturally discover itself in VISIONS. This is a species of fiction, to succeed in which with applause, requires as much poetic Inspiration as any other species of composition whatever. . . . it is the peculiar felicity of an original Author to feel in the most exquisite degree every emotion, and to see every scene he describes.

By the vigorous effort of a creative Imagination, he calls shadowy substances and unreal objects into existence. They are present to his view, and glide, like spectres, in silent, sullen majesty, before his astonished and intranced sight. In reading the description of such apparitions, we partake of the Author's emotion; the blood runs chill in our veins, and our hair stiffens with horror.[22]

I will not venture to guess how many people's hair actually stiffened with horror; it is enough to know that the reaction was considered possible, and that to the reader of the mid-eighteenth century personification was full of the highest poetic values, calling into fullest exercise the mind's noblest, most civilized faculty—the ability to generalize—thus enabling the reader to participate in community with the poet and other readers in the most elevated and sublime emotions.

IV *The Language of Generality*

Collins and his contemporaries, then, still considered the norm through which the reader approached poetry to be the universal concept, not the particular instance. Particulars fashion the universal, but have no poetic—that is, no *general* significance—unless seen in the context of a generality. The poet sought to express himself in terms no less powerful and all-encompassing than the laws of nature themselves, and we must remind ourselves of the great importance to all aspects of artistic theory and practice in the first half of the eighteenth century of the new scientific discoveries which tumbled one after another into the educated consciousness and which, with their apparent beautiful uniformity, strengthened the conviction that Truth and Beauty were really one, and that both depended upon the expression of universal and irrefutable verities. The personified abstraction, on one level, was an accurate linguistic means of expressing these truths; on another level, it was not a means by which to express any rational truth at all; it was, rather, the language of intense passion, as we have seen in the last quotation from Duff. Such passion, however, was often assumed to possess a visionary quality which, in its own way, possessed a higher truth.

In any case, the language of generality was a special one; and sometimes it sets up a special barrier for the twentieth-century reader, particularly if he has read the remarks of Wordsworth and Coleridge on eighteenth-century poetry, but has read little eighteenth-century poetry. The remarks on "poetic diction" are well known. What is not so generally recognized is that, if one is looking for poetic diction—and I shall attempt to define the term in a moment—he might well pursue a less fruitless search than to seek it in the poems of Wordsworth and Coleridge as well as in the best eighteenth-century verse.

I say the best eighteenth-century verse. The distinctions among the *kinds* of poetry are important to remember. The epistles, satires, occasional verse, and, for the most part, the elegies—that is, the best eighteenth-century verse—were as free from what Wordsworth and Coleridge were objecting to as the freest nineteenth-century poems. We have to search the pages of Pope very closely to find objectionable poetic diction which is not used satirically *as* diction. To this statement we must except the Homeric translations, to which *kind* the diction was considered appropriate and which set an unfortunate precedent for later attempts in the heroic style. In Pope's greatest works, however, one simply does not find the diction because it was not called for. In so far as the most vital *kinds* of eighteenth-century poetry were concerned, Pope, and Johnson after him, would have agreed emphatically with Wordsworth's statement that the languages of poetry and prose should be the same—a selection from the *real* language of men—and it is precisely on this point of view that Johnson's objections to Collins' verse are based.

The pastoral, georgic, and Pindarick *kinds*, however, were another matter; and it is important to remember, as Professor Tillotson so cogently points out, that as a whole these *kinds*, in which, so far as they survived, much of the greatest nineteenth-century poetry was written, were not the ones exploited most profitably by the eighteenth-century poets.[23] Pope's *Pastorals* can hardly be counted his greatest poems, and neither can *Windsor Forest*, though it is better by far than most of the later poems reminding us of it. Pope's St. Cecilia's Day Ode was recognized as inferior to Dryden's "Alexander's Feast," which was generally regarded as the greatest Pindarick by a modern. Except for the Pindaricks of Gray and Collins, there are no first-rate poems in this *kind* until we reach the nineteenth century, and there is very little neoclassic nature poetry which is first rate. *The Seasons* comes closest to what Wordsworth thought of, and what we have come to think of, as a nature poem; but it does not take much reflection to perceive that it is really something rather different from what Wordsworth or any other Romantic or post-Romantic attempted and should therefore be fairly judged on quite other grounds.

Judged on what grounds, so far as diction is concerned? In specific cases the defense is often easy. When Collins' in "Ode to Evening" writes "Then let me rove some wild and heathy scene," we may pick out "heathy" as an example of poetic diction and find that it grates on our ears. The question arises how Collins could have written more to the point. He is referring to a scene involving a heath. It is not, nor is it intended to be, a specific heath, evocation of which would be totally out of place in the economy of the poem, so particular illustrative details are not called for. Yet he is specifying. He is saying that, of all the various possibilities within the class "scenes," he is referring to the genus "pertaining to heaths." It is not appropriate to the intention of the poem nor to the verbal context that the scene be reduced to a species "Egdon Heath," just as we do not ordinarily need to specify when we say, "I enjoy mountain scenery," whether it be the Alps, the Rockies, or the Himalayas we have in mind. For purposes of the statement it is better not to specify. Collins in "heathy scene" wants to remind us of the general qualities associated with all heaths, in the same way as our statement about mountain scenery refers to those qualities which all mountains have in common. Collins' phrase, then, is perspicuous and concise, fulfilling with economy its purpose in the poem; it is, in effect, a kind of scientific-poetic language.

"But why," you may ask, "couldn't he just have said 'heath' "? Because it is not a heath as such which is important; it is the more general "scene" of which the heath is only the determining part. Again Collins' phrase is more precise, because it is not the responses to the heath—to the bogs and brambles—which are at issue; it is the response to the scene, in the same way that our response to mountain scenery is not to blistered heels or to poison oak but to something at least once removed from these.

"But," you say, objecting again, "one does not 'rove' a generalized scene; one roves a specific spot, in this case a heath." Collins is careful to say, however, *some* wild and heathy scene. There are many possibilities for roving in such a landscape, and for purposes of the poem—which we will examine later—it is important that we are not confined. It is the more general "scene" which is important; and, being the whole context of the scene which moves the poet at evening, it is literally and precisely, so far as the poem is concerned, the "scene" which he roves, not the heath itself. The determinant is the psychology of the poet, not the geography in which he finds himself.

That his sort of poetic diction has certain virtues of conciseness and precision may be illustrated by my having written an explication of one line somewhat longer than the poem in which it appears. It is generally true that the noun-plus-"y" kind of poetic diction can be defended on somewhat similar grounds. Mr. Arthos has shown the close association of this sort of phrase with scientific writing in the eighteenth century,[24] and, indeed, its use in poetry was intended to achieve a kind of scientific accuracy in description, even in such much-maligned periphrases as "finny tribe," in which, as Mr. Bateson has pointed out, the poet was specifying not just "fish," but fish considered solely as subjects for poetry, just as the scientists who invented the word "phlogistion" in 1733 were specifying not just the principle of inflammability, but that principle as used in the science of chemistry.[25]

Now it is true that such language is probably not the language of most men, no matter how vividly they see and feel. It is a special language for poetry, and a special defense of it might be made on the grounds that, as I think the eighteenth-century poets might have answered Wordsworth, most men do not write poetry. And those who do are attempting something at the same time more general and more precise with language for which the grosser terms of ordinary intercourse will not suffice. A watchmaker cannot use the tools of an iron founder, nor a surgeon the instruments of a hog-butcher; just so the poet cannot use their language—or, at least, the eighteenth-century poet could not.

Whether this idea is true *sub specie aeternitatis* it is not the business of historical criticism to decide. We today would not be so sure of its truth, but for our present purposes it is enough to point out that the eighteenth century was quite sure of it, although there were changes and disagreements as to the application of the idea. Mr. Bateson distinguishes two theories of poetic diction during the eighteenth century, which he calls negative and positive; and he says it is only to the latter that the term "poetic diction" should properly be applied.[26] The negative theory, predominant in the early century, said that there were certain words which, for reasons which we will examine in a moment, were not suitable to be used in poetry. The positive theory was stated by Gray when he wrote to West:

As to matter of stile, I have this to say: The language of the age is never the language of poetry; except among the French, whose verse, where thought or image does not support it, differs in nothing from prose. Our poetry, on the contrary, has a language peculiar to itself; to which almost every one, that has written, has added something by enriching it with foreign idioms and derivatives: Nay sometimes words of their own composition or invention. Shakespear and Milton have been great creators this way; and no one more licentious than Pope or Dryden, who perpetually borrow expressions from the former. . . . And our language not being a settled thing (like the French) has an undoubted right to words of an hundred years old, provided antiquity have not rendered them unintelligible.[27]

In other words, Gray thought that there was a special "poetic" language for English, composed at least in part of archaisms and neologisms. It was to Gray's sort of language, and to personifications and other highly rhetorical figures, that Wordsworth objected.

About this second, "positive" kind of poetic language there is little I need say. Such specially "poetic" words as Collins uses are obvious enough and not troublesome to readers brought up on Romantic poetry. But I think Collins' diction is illuminated by considering some of the words he might have used but did not: that is, Mr. Bateson's "negative" poetic diction. For, however Collins may sometimes have used tortured syntax and strained metaphors, his diction is generally conservative.[28]

For the conservative point of view I will again quote Joseph Warton, who laments in the Preface to his translation of the *Georgics*

[81]

. . . the meanness of the terms of husbandry is concealed and lost in a dead language, and they convey no low or despicable image to the mind; but the coarse and common words I was necessitated to use in the following translation, viz. *plough and sow, wheat, dung, ashes, horse and cow* &c., will, I fear, unconquerably disgust many a delicate reader, if he doth not make proper allowances for a modern compared with an ancient language. . . .[29]

There are some words which should not be used in poetry because they are not to readers' tastes, but this is not owing to the hyper-delicacy which is at first sight implied. I think that the aim of the exclusion was positive: it was to exclude certain words because, by doing so, the poet could gain particular effects which were not otherwise possible. The "mean" word was to be excluded not because it was common—obviously most words the poet uses must come from the word-hoard of daily communication—but because it was imprecise: the connotation of a "mean" word was such that it obscured the poet's primary meaning. The poetry of the Augustans was a poetry of statement. The writers of the late seventeenth and early eighteenth centuries were acutely conscious of the rhetorical confusions which had accompanied and, in part, precipitated the revolution; and the search for a precise English vocabulary to meet the needs of increasing scientific knowledge was carried over into a search for a literary vocabulary which would be just as pure and express an idea as clearly and be as free from connotation as a mathematical equation.

By Collins' time obscurity-sublimity was admitted into poetry on less specialized occasions than had been the case in Dryden's lifetime, but the techniques for achieving the emotional charge were still essentially the same: through syntactical manipulation and evocation of personified emotions, not as was the case with Donne and is today, by deliberate use of ambivalent language. The "mean" word was banned in the sort of poetry Collins wrote because it brought to mind associations irrelevant to the primary meaning of the poem. In other sorts of poetry, as I have indicated, the vocabulary was free. Pope uses in his original poems every one of the words Warton bemoaned except "wheat," but he uses them in his epistles, satires, and poetical essays, where the restrictions were much less rigid than in other *kinds.* "Ashes" is used only in the "Elegy to an Unfortunate Lady"—an obvious context—but

Pope clearly felt no limitation of vocabulary applied to the other *kinds*. It is interesting, though, that none of these bucolic words appears in his *Pastorals*.

I have encountered no more concise and clear exposition of the dangers of "mean" words than that appearing in James Beattie's "Illustrations on Sublimity," from which I have already quoted and from which I should like to quote another passage with a few interspersed comments. Remember that Beattie is speaking only of that poetry which aims to be "sublime": "Those words are not mean, which are so necessary at all times, that it is impossible to speak without them on any subject. And most of the classical words in every tongue are of this character. Words are not mean, because they are plain; nor elegant, because none but men of learning understand them: on the contrary, every thing in style is blameable, which is obscure or ambiguous to an attentive reader." We note here that in language obscurity and ambiguity are blameable, although Beattie elsewhere commends obscurity as an essential attribute of sublimity.

. . . Uncommon expressions are in general to be avoided, where they can be avoided. It is pedantry to affect them. And therefore, we must not imagine, that words are mean, or not elegant, merely because they are common.

But secondly; Many words there are in every tongue, which are not used, except by illiterate persons, or on very familiar occasions, or in order to express what the decorum of polite society requires that we conceal: and these may be called *mean words;* and are never to be introduced in sublime description, in elegant writing, or on any solemn or serious topick.

Such, in the first place, are vulgar proverbs. These, though they may have a good meaning, are too familiar to find a place in good style. . . .

Common forms of compliment, though innocent in themselves, and though in society agreeable, because customary, must not appear in elegant writing: first because they are too familiar to the ear, being used on every trivial occasion; and secondly, because they derive their meaning from the manners of particular times and places.

Beattie saw no conflict between the idea that language must be unambiguous and the idea that certain expressions must be proscribed as deriving their meaning "from the manners of particular times and places" because there was to his mind no such conflict. The particular times and places impart specialized connotations which obscure the clear, single meaning of the word.

[Third] are those idioms, commonly called *cant;* a jargon introduced by ignorant or affected persons, and which the most perfect acquaintance with every good author in a language would not enable one to understand. . . . To say, of a person, whose conversation is tedious, that he is a *bore;* of a drunk man that he is *in liquor* . . . that he *has his load* . . . ; of one, who has nothing to reply, that he is *dumbfounded;* of a transaction committed to writing, that it is taken down in *black and white;* of a person baffled in any enterprise . . . that he is *routed horse foot and dragoons;* . . . of one, who has enriched himself by any business, that he has *feather'd his nest:*—these, and the like idioms are all cant . . . and polite writers and speakers, unless they mean to speak or write ludicrously, avoid them as vulgarities of the lowest order.

With this proscription I think most of us would agree today. Beattie next condemns words peculiar to the vocabulary of a group or profession:

partly because, being technical, they have something of a vulgar appearance; and chiefly, because to the greater part of readers they are unintelligible. . . .

It is scarce necessary to add, that all phrases are mean, which come under the denomination of barbarism, or provincial idiom; because they suggest the ideas of vulgar things, and illiterate persons. Meanness blended with dignity is one of those incongruities that provoke laughter.[30]

Spread out before us like this, the rules may seem less restrictive and more sensible than a mere statement of them might lead us to believe. I do not see that the exclusions impoverished the poetry; the bad effect they did have was to lead some poets to attempt, in an effort to avoid particular "mean" words, periphrases whch were beyond their abilities to carry off without becoming ridiculous. But this was a failure of the poet's talents, not a deficiency in the theory. In neither Collins nor Gray, and surprisingly seldom in the great bulk of Thomson's work, does a restrictive rule lead the poet to any violation of his intention or of our sensibilities.

The question of diction, however, must not be confused with the question of how the vocabulary is used. Collins' vocabulary, as I said, is conservative. He was content to write within the Augustan confines, even though his sensibility was not in every respect Augustan, and although he apparently did not consider himself to belong to the Augustan age. His idiom, however, is neither quite conventional even within the *kind* of the sublime Pindarick nor within the forms of ordinary social intercourse; it was to Collins' idiom, essentially, that Johnson objected when he wrote: ". . . his diction was often harsh, unskilfully laboured, and injudiciously selected. He affected the obsolete when it was not worthy of revival; and he puts his words out of the common order, seeming to think, with some later candidates for fame, that not to write prose is certainly to write poetry." [31]

Johnson, not by any means idiosyncratically, hated anything which smacked of affection and held, as had Dryden and Pope, that the basis of any metrical composition must be the idiom of educated speech in cultivated society. In so far as Collins violated this idiom, he fell foul of Johnson, who, however, had had to admit that "as diligence is never wholly lost, if his efforts sometimes caused harshness and obscurity, they likewise produced in happier moments sublimity and splendour"—which, after all, is exactly what Collins was trying to achieve.

V *The Sympathetic Imagination*

If a luxuriance of imagination, a wild sublimity of fancy, and a felicity of expression so extraordinary that it might be supposed to be suggested by some superior power—if these are allowed to constitute the excellence of lyric poetry, the author of the *Odes descriptive and allegorical* will indisputably bear away the palm from all his competitors in that province of the muse.

That critique of Collins was published in the *Monthly Review* for January 1764 (21), and marks the beginning of wide acclaim for his talents. I do not know quite what readers of poetry would agree upon today as constituting the excellence of lyric poetry; probably no very wide area of agreement could be found. If we could agree, our criteria would certainly not be couched in the terms quoted above. Yet those are terms which we must accept if we are going to be fair to Collins' poetry, and fairness is possible only in so far as we can read it through the understandings of his contemporaries.

We probably cannot overturn the customs of a lifetime in order to read a poet, but I have tried to point out in this chapter some of the readjustments of apprehension which a sympathetic twentieth-century reader of Collins must attempt to make if he wishes to see what the poet was trying to do and to judge on some historically valid ground how well he succeeded. No doubt even the most scholarly and best-willed readers will to some extent fail, for the imagination of the eighteenth century is probably so far away from ours that we can never glimpse it except dimly. "Teach me but once like Him to *feel*," Collins wrote of Shakespeare, and we could say the same of Collins. It is a legitimate cry, for his poetry was meant to be felt; and it is just there that our sympathies most often fail to touch his.

Our world is not his, and no amount of thinking will make it so, yet we today still entertain at least unconsciously the eighteenth-century notion that all men at all times and places—or, the anthropologist would amend severely, within a single cultural tradition—are subject to the same human feelings. Man, in other words, is a universal constant. But who knows whether this be true or not? None of us has ever lived and felt except by imaginative extension in a time other than his own. But certainly the occasions for the emotions can differ, and men can at different times be stirred by different things. These truisms we will all admit. Let us be ready to admit, then, if the grandeur and "sublimity" of generality could stir men two hundred years ago, that their emotion may have been as genuine as ours on a different occasion. Perhaps by this exercise we may even extend our own sympathies; we may even end up enjoying Collins.

CHAPTER 3

The Poems Themselves

IF WE are going to enjoy Collins' poetry, we must read it; for any commentary can be but supplementary. Fortunately for the weary or reluctant who may be chilled by this pronouncement, the body of Collins' verse is very small and the proportion of good poems is high. One can read Collins' entire *œuvre* carefully in at most a few hours, and the rewards will be great.

There are no problems about the chronology of Collins' poems with which we need concern ourselves here, and the textual problems are either simple or unsolvable. The Oxford edition is easily come by. It is reading Collins' poems, not this book, which may open the door to such pleasures as those poems can give.

I   *The Early Poems*

In the later years of the eighteenth century Collins' fame was based upon the "wildness" of his imagination, the extravagance of his imagery. There were "frequent public recitations" of "The Passions." I do not know that this element in his poetry could have been forecast by a reader of his earliest verses, certainly not by readers of the *Persian Eclogues* or the *Verses Humbly Address'd to Sir Thomas Hanmer*. Before I discuss these, however, I should like to return to the little "Sonnet" ("When *Phœbe* . . .") which I have already mentioned as being perhaps Collins' earliest poem, or at least one of his earliest, and the only poem of unchallenged authenticity written before the *Eclogues*. It is so short it will be convenient to quote it:

> When *Phœbe* form'd a wanton smile,
>   My soul! it reach'd not here!
> Strange, that thy peace, thou trembler, flies
>   Before a rising tear!

From midst the drops, my love is born,
 That o'er those eyelids rove:
Thus issued from a teeming wave
 The fabled queen of love.

As a schoolboy poem these verses are remarkable, particularly coming from the 1730's, when the minor poets of the seventeenth century were largely ignored. It would be pleasant to be able to prove that Collins had gotten so far beyond the confines of the Winchester curriculum as to have begun exploring earlier English literature on his own; we could thereby account for the conceit in the second stanza in terms of an imitation of one of the Cavaliers. It probably is such an imitation, but I do not know the source of it, if any; and, because we totally lack information as to Collins' intellectual life apart from his formal studies, which did not include English poetry, we can only infer that he was turning over a library in his spare hours. Was this at Joseph Warton's instigation? Again we can only make inferences; but, since the known friendship between Joseph Warton and Collins is the easiest way to account for many things in Collins' intellectual life, there is no reason to deny Joseph Warton an important part in his friend's career, particularly in these early years, when the son of the erudite schoolmaster would very likely be leading the hatter's son, and leading him, it appears, on lines predictable from our knowledge of the learnèd father.

All this is perhaps too much to draw from eight lines for which I should like to account more fully than I can. Within their limitations the lines are exceedingly good. It is not clear how in the first stanza the smile becomes a rising tear until we realize that "wanton" means "willful" or "willed" through the tears. The smile is not what affects the soul; it is still the tears to which the poet responds. The second stanza seems to me a gem with its charming reminiscence of the legend of Venus. The modern reader may be stopped momentarily by the "teeming wave" until he realizes that the image is literally accurate in terms of the legend. "Teeming" was not yet, apparently, a purely poetic word, as reference to the *Oxford English Dictionary* will indicate. The poem has the tightness and depth of reverberation of the metaphysicals rather than the decorative surface of most early eighteenth-century lyrics.

Had there been many poets writing thus, the 1730's might be remembered for lyrics as well as for Pope.

As I mentioned in the first chapter, there is nothing in "When *Phœbe* . . ." which would lead us to anticipate the *Persian Eclogues,* so titled upon their first publication in 1742, or the *Oriental Eclogues,* as they were called when republished with minor revisions in 1757 and as they have generally been known since. They soon seem to have acquired a modest fame and were, ironically, the only poems by which Collins was well known during his lifetime. I say "ironically" because they are hardly poems which would be much noted today if Collins had not written them, pleasant though they are. Goldsmith in 1759 spoke of "The neglected author of the *Persian Eclogues,* which, however inaccurate, excel any in our language . . . ," [1] and he seems to have been reflecting a fairly general opinion.

In 1742 Pope was still very much alive. By publishing these poems, the young Oxford student was entering into direct competition with the poet acknowledged to be the living master of this form. I do not know that we need to look for any direct influences; echoes of Pope's *Pastorals* are surely not hard to find; there are quite a number of direct parallels,[2] but for the most part the echoes are inherent in the mere act of writing this sort of poetry. We could expect to find more hints as to influences in the Oriental vogue of the time, but that also is too indefinite for us to trace. Warton seems to provide the best clue:

Mr. Collins wrote his eclogues when he was about seventeen years old, at Winchester school, and, as I well remember, had been just reading that volume of Salmon's Modern History, which described Persia; which determined him to lay the scene of these pieces [there], as being productive of new images and sentiments. In his maturer years he was accustomed to speak very contemptuously of them, calling them his Irish Eclogues, and they had in them not one spark of Orientalism; and desiring me to erase a motto he had prefixed to them in a copy he gave me;—quos primus equis oriens afflavit anhelis. Virg. He was greatly mortified that they found more readers and admirers than his odes.[3]

Salmon on Persia is very tame stuff. W. C. Bronson points out that "although sensible and mildly interesting, [it] is not imaginative or picturesque; and Collins showed he was greatly athirst by sucking from it as much romance as he did." [4] Even for that amount of romance Collins was careful to apologize in the Preface:

There is an Elegancy and Wildness of Thought which recommends all their [the Persians'] Compositions; and our Genius's are as much too cold for the Entertainment of such Sentiments, as our Climate is for their Fruits and Spices. If any of these Beauties are to be found in the following *Eclogues* I hope my Reader will consider them as an Argument of their being Original. . . .

Whatever Defects, as, I doubt not, there will be many, fall under the Reader's Observation, I hope his Candour will incline him to make the following Reflection:

That the Works of *Orientals* contain many Peculiarities, and that through Defect of Language few *European* Translators can do them Justice.   (1757 ed.)

There is certainly "elegancy" in Collins' poems, but the "wildness" eludes us, except perhaps momentarily in the second and fourth eclogues. Collins was quite right, also, in recognizing in his later years that the poems are not Oriental (though exactly what denigration he intended by calling them "Irish" is not clear), but they were as Oriental as most of the other products of that vogue in the 1730's. That Salmon was his major source is quickly confirmed by reference to that not very sprightly work. The following passages, for example, evidently account for a good deal of what Collins writes in the Preface and in the first eclogue:

Every great man has a poet in his family, and no entertainment is complete unless a poet be there to oblige the company with his compositions. There are many of them who frequent the coffee-houses, and publick places of resort, where they repeat their poems to the audience, and are sent for even by the common people to their houses on solemn occasions, in imitation, probably of their surperiors, for the King himself entertains several as his domesticks . . .

Their poets are very nice as to the rhime, but something negligent in their numbers. According to the Persians, the antient philosophers in the east were all poets, and their lessons were delivered in verse . . . The Subject of their poems is generally some piece of morality, or philosophy.

[90]

Poetry seems to be a talent peculiar to the Persians, in which they excell more than in any other part of literature. Their invention is fruitful and lively, their manner sweet, their temper amorous, and their language has a softness proper to verse . . . The thoughts are noble and elevated . . . their allusions are delicate, and abundance of hyperbole you must expect in all their figures. Love is sometimes the subject of their poems, as well as morality and history; but nothing immodest, or that countenances debauchery of any kind, is ever the subject of their verse.[5]

So there is basis for some of the Orientalism, and Collins took a number of details from Salmon in addition to the jonquils which he himself footnotes in the third eclogue—notably many of the details in the second and the historical background in the fourth. But sources do not really matter, for it is very unlikely that it ever occurred to anyone at the time to expect or want the poems to be "realsitic" or to present anything of what Persian or pastoral life was really like. Not many years later Johnson could fulminate against the pastoral on grounds of its artificiality, but at the time Collins wrote, the pastoral was accepted as a form as artificial as the sonata, and was to be appreciated in very much the same way. Collins went further than most writers of pastorals in introducing "realism" into his work, but whether this is one of its merits is doubtful. The chief merit is, as Mackail says, "an unequalled limpidity and a delicate sweetness." [6] If anyone doubts that the heroic couplet is capable of poetic music, let him turn to Collins' pastorals, or, for that matter, to Pope's. The pentameter couplet was a medium that Collins had mastered before he was twenty, but which he was to use only once again, with equal technical ability, though with a less fortunate subject, in the *Epistle to Hanmer*.

The *Persian Eclogues* scarcely need detailed explication; their sentiments are neither particularly subtle nor profound, and they can be read and enjoyed (if we approach them with no preconceived antipathy) just for what they are and on their own terms: as eighteenth-century poems of a pleasing sort. Yet there are a few comments one may make.

In the first eclogue, although, as we have seen, there was some justification in Salmon for having Selim sing to the Persian maids on moral themes, we may feel that we are too nearly reading a versification of one of Richardson's *Letters*. The first is certainly to us the weakest of the four poems, yet it may not have seemed so to Collins' readers. When he writes, for example,

> Blest were the Days, when Wisdom held her Reign,
> And Shepherds sought her on the silent Plain,
> With Truth she wedded in the secret Grove,
> Immortal TRUTH, and Daughters bless'd their Love.   (43-46)

he is appealing to several very powerful interests of the time. The interest in the Golden Age, inherited from the Renaissance and remotest antiquity, and implied in the social theories of Locke and the most forward-looking of eighteenth-century social philosophers, was a conventional part of the pastoral. Collins could not have avoided it had he wanted to, and his readers would have been distressed had it not appeared in the poems. At the same time the marriage of Wisdom and Truth producing the Virtues (as it does in the next few lines) puts in personified form the idea that virtue is finally rational, another of the stock ideas of the age. Naturally, however, the Virtues can operate only in a society of peace and plenty, an idea which Collins is to mention again in his odes; and, we must remember, peace and plenty are the ideals of the commercial society in which Collins was reared and lived. This passage, conventional though it is—and partly because of its conventionality in both the good and bad connotations of the word—struck deeply into the social organism of which its author was a part, just as the personifications of Modesty and Chastity in the next few lines evoked the ideal "manners" of the time. They were goddesses to whom society bowed, whether or not that society obeyed their commands any more than does ours today. Respect was due them in the eighteenth century no less than it is due today to our goddesses Unconventionality or Psychology.

The second eclogue, "Hassan; or, the Camel-Driver," is more striking, and possibly the best of the four, although I am undecided whether to prefer Hassan in his desert waste or Agib and Secander on their mountain in Circassia in the last eclogue. In both of these, the verse has the vigor genuinely to evoke some imaginative sympathy on our part:

> At that dead Hour the silent Asp shall creep,
> If ought of rest I find, upon my Sleep:
> Or some swoln Serpent twist his Scales around,
> And wake to Anguish with a burning Wound.
> Thrice happy they, the wise contended Poor,
> From Lust of Wealth, and Dread of Death secure!
> They tempt no Desarts, and no Griefs they find;
> Peace rules the Day, where Reason rules the Mind.
> *Sad was the Hour, and luckless was the Day,*
> *When first from Schiraz' Walls I bent my Way!*   (61-70)

The "wise contented Poor" remind us momentarily of Gray's "short and simple annals" in his *Elegy* and of the inhabitants of Goldsmith's Sweet Auburn. The idea, of course, was another conventional one in Collins' age, closely tied in with the primitivistic touch in the first eclogue, which Collins was to make central in one of the best parts of the "Ode on the Popular Superstitions of the Highlands," his last poem. The whole of "Hassan" is concerned with the lament at being betrayed by the search for gold, but that this idea was inconsistent with the objectives of a commercial society never seems to have disturbed anyone.

In "Abra; or, the Georgian Sultana," the third eclogue, we have the story of the shepherdess who is found and married by the emperor Abbas but still retains her pastoral simplicity:

> Yet midst the Blaze of Courts she fix'd her Love,
> On the cool Fountain, or the shady Grove;
> Still with the Shepherd's Innocence her Mind
> To the sweet Vale, and flow'ry Mead inclin'd.   (37-40)

There are several possible analogues to this story, but no clear source. Mr. Ainsworth suggests the story of Nour Mahal recounted in Salmon on *The Present State of Proper India;* W. C. Bronson says Collins may have invented it himself. There is no reason for us to worry; the story has the true pastoral flavor, and that alone eliminates the problem of originality.

"Agib and Secander; or, the Fugitives" presents a conversation between these two unfortunates at midnight on a mountain in Circassia. This is Collins' most original touch in the *Oriental Ec-*

logues; for, while Spenser and others had used the pastoral form as the vehicle for social comment, the form in the eighteenth century had become so prettified that it took an original mind to return, however tentatively, to the earlier patterns. Did Collins know Spenser's *Shepheardes Calendar?* I am willing to guess that he may have, though there is no proof. Certainly in Collins' fourth eclogue there is no more than the most tentative and generalized hint of social purpose:

> Unhappy Land, whose Blessings tempt the Sword,
> In vain, unheard, thou call'st thy *Persian* Lord!
> In vain thou court'st him, helpless to thine Aid,
> To shield the Shepherd, and protect the Maid!
> Far off in thoughtless Indolence resign'd,
> Soft dreams of Love and Pleasure sooth his Mind:
> 'Midst fair *Sultanas* lost in idle Joy,
> No Wars alarm him, and no Fears annoy.   (31-38)

And later on there is even a call to what might very rashly be called rebellion:

> Ye *Georgian* Swains that piteous learn from far
> *Circassia's* Ruin, and the Waste of War:
> Some weightier Arms than Crooks and Staves prepare,
> To shield your Harvests, and defend your Fair:
> The *Turk* and *Tartar* like Designs pursue,
> Fix'd to destroy, and stedfast to undo.   (59-64)

The whole of the last eclogue is vigorous and manly, without that hint of weariness which colors the second. Reading the four poems we can only be surprised at the precocity of the youth who wrote them, but we must remember that we do not know what they were first like or what processes of revision they went through before publication.

Collins' practices in revision are most evident from the two versions we possess of the *Verses . . . to Sir Thomas Hanmer,* published first in December, 1743, and considerably revised and republished the next year under the title *An Epistle: Addrest to Sir Thomas Hanmer*—considerably revised and shortened by ten lines, but not much improved. Of several essays in the epistle Collins published only this one, unless we wish to consider the "Ode on the Popular Superstitions of the Highlands of Scotland" as belonging to this *kind*. The others have recently been found and published,[7] and they show Collins to have been just as ill at ease in the traditional form of the *kind* as the Hanmer poem suggests.

Not that *Hanmer* is bad as eighteenth-century epistolary poems go. A comparison with similar verses in the 1755 *Collection* by Dodsley, who reprinted Collins' epistle, shows it to be at least equal to any of the others, and far better than most of them—modest enough praise. But, after all, there was Pope. Collins could meet Pope quite successfully on his own ground in the pastoral, but in the epistle the brilliance of Pope puts anyone else in English in deepest shadow. Pope has made it impossible for anyone following him to write this *kind* of poem, perhaps for as long as our language remains in its modern form. Whatever Collins' talents were, and they were certainly very considerable, they were not the talents of a Pope, even though there are in Collins occasional lines which have the silver ring:

> Each rising Art by just Gradation moves,
> Toil builds on Toil, and Age on Age improves.
> The Muse alone unequal dealt her Rage,
> And grac'd with noblest Pomp her earliest Stage.
> (1743: 29-32)

These lines, voicing one of the continuing themes of Collins' poetry, must have met his approval because they appear unchanged in the second version of the poem. They have the sound but not quite the wit of Pope. They are not bad; in fact, they are good—but they are not brilliant, and after Pope nothing less than brilliance will do.

The lines quoted indicate that the poem is a "progress piece," one like Gray's "Progress of Poesy," which takes us through the author's conception of the history of poetry. Even in this respect Collins' poem is somewhat disappointing, for his view of the progress of poetry is not remarkable either for penetration or originality, though it shows a pretty scholarship. He uses the "progress" in truncated form again in the odes to Fear and Simplicity; and, among the fragments of verse resurrected by Mr. Cunningham,

there are forty-five lines, possibly intended for the *Epistle to Hanmer,* which discuss the restoration drama. In these latter verses we
find the complaint about the stage dominated by art rather than
nature and by France rather than by the native genius of the English theater:

> Those courtly Wits which spoke the Nation's voice
> In Paris learn'd their judgment and their choice
> Vain were the Thoughts, which Nature's Passions speak,
> Thy woes Monimia Impotent and weak!
> Vain all the Truth of just Dramatic Tales!
> Nought pleas'd Augustus, but what pleased Versailles! [8]

It is interesting to observe that Collins did not consider himself an
"Augustan," but speaks of "Augustus" as if in the distant past.

In *Hanmer,* as I have said, we do not find Collins' remarks
particularly penetrating. The praises of Shakespeare are such as
might have been uttered by almost anyone at the time, even to the
idea that Shakespeare is useful as a moralist: "Whate'er the
Wounds this youthful Heart shall feel, / Thy Songs support me,
and thy Morals heal!" (1744: 105-6). There is also some emphasis,
which concerns us in the light of what Collins was later to do in
the *Odes,* on the pictorial quality in Shakespeare:

> O might some Verse with happiest Skill persuade
> Expressive Picture to adopt thine Aid!
> What wond'rous Draughts might rise from ev'ry Page!
> What other *Raphaels* Charm a distant Age! (1744: 109-12)

He proceeds then for twenty lines to describe two pictures which
might be drawn: Antony over the corpse of Caesar, and Volumnia
pleading with Coriolanus. Both of these give ample opportunity
for the heroic, posed gesture; the flowing drapery; and the pa-
thetic expressions found in Hellenistic and later statuary, the most
admired (because the only known) Classical art. I shall have
more to say of Collins' obvious interest in this art later on, but we
may notice it as an interest already manifest. The particular turn
of the interest may be, perhaps, discerned from one of Collins' revisions of the 1743 edition of *Hanmer.* In the first edition Collins
writes of Volumnia: "The frantic Mother leads their wild despair, /

Beats her swoln Breast, and rends her silver Hair." (1743: 109-10). This might do for a painting, as Collins says, but we may suspect it is not really a painting Collins visualizes when he revises these lines to: "See the fond Mother 'midst the plaintive Train/Hung on his Knees, and prostrate on the Plain!" (1744: 129-30).

I prefer the first version myself, but I think I can see what is behind Collins' revision. The second version is much more static, more statuesque, more posed (how can anyone be posed both beating her breast and tearing her hair? The line is a cinema shot, not a painting). If it is a painting, it is one by Poussin, and the pose is also right for a statue carved in the pyramidal form of academic art. Indeed, it is one of the praises Collins bestows on Hanmer's edition that "Thus, gen'rous Critic, as thy Bard inspires,/The Sister Arts shall nurse their drooping Fires" (1744: 135-6).

The chief virtue of the *Epistle* is the negative one that Collins was not fulsome in praise of Hanmer. There are only eight lines at the beginning of the poem and ten at the end devoted to this obvious duty. Perhaps eighteen lines out of one hundred fifty was not considered enough. At any rate, Collins seems to have derived no benefit from Hanmer, and very little from anyone else. The second edition, as I have remarked, first brought Collins' name before the public, and was a not an inappropriate occasion upon which to publish the *Song from Cymbeline*.

Why Collins chose to write a song inviting direct comparison with one of Shakespeare's best is an interesting question, but not one to which we are likely to find an answer. Collins' song is full of reminiscences of "Fear no more the heat o'th'sun" and of preceding lines from Act IV, Scene ii, of *Cymbeline;*[9] and it could, lacking anything else, be used in place of Shakespeare's song, though surely no one has ever so used it. (Johnson, as a tribute to his friend, appended the song to his edition of the play.) It is a pleasant song, but the eighteenth-century "melting Virgins" and "breathing Spring" do not fit into Shakespeare's play. What it amounts to is that Collins was touched by this sentimental (in the good sense of the term) scene and by it and, on some unknown occasion, was inspired to write the song. That of all Shakespeare it should have been this scene which so inspired him is no doubt significant, but I do not think that, lacking any information about an occasion for the song or the circumstances of its composition, we are entitled to dwell very much upon this significance. It is not the sort of scene in which Collins anywhere else—in *Hanmer* or in the odes to "Pity" and "Fear"—shows himself particularly interested, another reason for passing lightly over the possible importance this song might have as particularly indicative of Collins' dramatic tastes. W. C. Bronson states that "the inspiration of the line was a fine sympathy with the spirit of Shaskespere's scene as a whole";[10] the song seems to me to rest upon a total misconception of the scene as a whole—but a misconception perfectly in accord with the taste of the 1740's and entirely explicable by reference to the then current interpretations of Shakespeare. From our standpoint, I think, Collins would have done better to have let the song stand without any reference to Shakespeare at all.

II   *The Odes: The Book Itself*

No one could have foretold in 1744 that two years later Collins would publish one of the most remarkable little volumes of poetry of the century. The only hint which a phenomenally foresighted reader might have had was contained in "When *Phœbe* . . . ," and that, could it have been interpreted, would probably have been misleading. By somewhat stretching our hindsight, we can detect the vaguest hints in the *Persian Eclogues* and even in *Hanmer*. "Wildering Fear" and "desp'rate Sorrow" in the eighth line of the fourth eclogue, particularly "wildering Fear," have something of the touch; and the "shriller Shriek" at the end of the same poem anticipates a famous phrase in "Ode to Evening." But even with the total work before us, the transition from the poems I have discussed to those I am about to consider is inexplicable except on the one ground that an historical critic is never safe in attempting to penetrate, that of genius. We can find the biographical stimulus for the patriotic odes; we can assume with considerable assurance that Collins' study of Aristotle for his proposed translation of the *Poetics* with commentary stimulated him to write "Pity" and "Fear"; we can find analogues for "On the Poetical Character" and trace the concepts behind "Simplicity." Some of these poems are better than others, and one or two of the poems in the 1746 volume[11] are simply not very good; but nothing

Collins had previously done could have led anyone to anticipate or, so far as I can see, can help us to explain the total effect of the volume. And, particularly, nothing can account for the perfection of "Ode to Evening" and "How Sleep the Brave" and for the memorable qualities of "Liberty" and "The Passions."

The volume is one of the rarest of books. Millar printed a thousand copies, but, we know, the sale was disappointing, and Langhorne records that Collins bought back those unsold and burned them. Probably the few who did buy the book were not particularly careful to preserve it. It was "exceedingly rare" at the time of Wordsworth's death. Professor Garrod has complained that it is "badly printed, very badly punctuated, and, in respect of its contents, ill arranged." [12] I do not know which copy Professor Garrod saw, but of books two hundred years old which I have examined, I should say that Collins' is one of the pleasanter examples. The type is large and clear, the margins are ample (even in the trimmed British Museum copy), the disposition of type upon the page is attractive. Collins should have been proud of his book as a book; it is a much better job of bookmaking than Dodsley did for Joseph Warton. As to whether it is badly punctuated, that we shall see. It is not punctuated by twentieth-century standards. Nor am I certain that in respect to contents it is ill-arranged. I will not particularly defend the arrangement, which, incidentally, the Oxford edition follows; it may be inconvenient for purposes of interpreting the odes in some preconceived scheme or for arriving inductively at an interpretation of the volume as a single poetical unit. But I do not see that we are absolutely obliged to interpret the volume as a single poetical unit. It is a book of poems, not a poem.

On the other hand, there is some case to be made for the arrangement as it stands. The book opens with three odes on the constituent emotions of poetry: Pity, Fear, and Simplicity, and follows these with a generalized treatment "On the Poetical Character." These poems make an intelligible unit. There follow four "patriotic" or political odes: "Written in the Beginning of the Year 1746" (which I have more conveniently referred to as "How Sleep the Brave"), odes to Mercy and Liberty, and the ode "To a Lady on the Death of Colonel Ross in the Action of Fontenoy." These also cohere. The last four odes, "To Evening," "Peace," "The Manners" and "The Passions, an Ode for Music" are less integrated as a unit and have thus led to Professor Garrod's accusation. Evening is the time of peace, the aspect which by implication is stressed in the poem; and the "Ode to Peace," arising perhaps from this aspect, follows the "Ode to Evening" as naturally as it would precede it. It is, however, another political poem. "The Manners" and the ode on "The Passions" are both poems about poetry, the first about the relation of the poet to his world, the second a most appropriate concluding cry for the passions ennobling the poetry of the Ancients and Milton to come dwell among the inhabitants of the present "laggard Age."

We are not obliged to interpret *Odes on Several Descriptive and Allegoric Subjects* as though it were one volume attempting to be a coherent whole, but I think that it generally coheres much better than most volumes of poetry. Mr. Musgrove has, on the premise of such coherence, suggested an interpretation which makes the book as a whole to be about "the nature of the True Poet," [13] and I believe he is essentially correct in his interpretation, even though it may be somewhat Procrustean. I shall return to Mr. Musgrove's article after I have discussed the poems. The book may be ill-arranged, but I think it shows clear evidence of conscious arrangement; and, after all, it is the book we have which we must talk about, not the book as we should like it to have been.

III *The Odes:*
Pity, Fear, Simplicity, The Poetical Character

The book as we have it opens with the odes to Pity and Fear, the Aristotelian emotions. I do not know how Collins was planning to translate the crucial passage in the *Poetics* about pity and fear, but it is interesting that the only translation readily available to him in the early eighteenth century handles the famous definition of tragedy somewhat differently than modern translators. *Aristotle's Art of Poetry. Translated from the original GREEK, according to Mr. Theodore Goulston's Edition,* 1705, renders the definition as follows: "Tragedy is then, an Imitation of an Action that is Grave, Entire, and hath a Just Length; of which the Stile is agreeably relishing, but differently in all its parts; and which without the assistance of Narration, by means of Compassion and

Terror perfectly refines in us, all sorts of Passions, and whatever else is like them." In the Comment, translated from Dacier, we find some further illumination:

. . . the *Peripateticks* being perswaded that 'twas only the Excess was Vitious, and that the Passions when regulated were useful, nay necessary, they meant only, by *To Refine the Passions*, to Curb the Excess, by which they err'd, and to reduce them to a Just Moderation. . . . It excites them then, by setting before our Eyes, the Calamities, into which, those who are like ourselves, have fallen by involuntary Faults; and it refines them, by rendring those very Misfortunes, familiar to us, because it teaches us by that, not to fear them, nor to be too much Concern'd when they do really happen to us.[14]

What Collins would have done with the concept ordinarily translated today as "purgation" or "catharsis" which appears in this 1705 translation as "refines in us" we have no way of knowing. The idea "refines in us," however, seems more in accord with what Collins wrote in the two Aristotelian odes. It helps to explain the exclamation "And I, O Fear, will dwell with Thee!" at the end of the "Ode to Fear," and it also provides a double meaning for the opening of "Ode to Pity":

> O THOU, the Friend of Man assign'd
> With balmy Hands his wounds to bind,
> And charm his frantic Woe. . . .

It is not only the personified Pity who binds the wounds, but also the personified Tragic Pity. That something of the sort may have been in Collins' mind is further suggested by the conclusion, when it is clearly the Tragic Pity with whom in her temple the poet asks to dwell and

> There waste the mournful Lamp of Night
> Till, Virgin, Thou again delight
> To hear a *British* Shell!   (40-43)

The poem is a tribute to Euripides and Otway as well as a lament that, since the time of Otway, Tragic Pity is no more to be found in England.

Pity here is less vividly visualized than some of Collins' other personifications; the most vivid part of the poem is the description of the temple of Pity, and Thomas Warton, with that engaging solicitude for one another which all the Wartons had, reports it as his opinion that "In the *Ode to Pity,* the idea of a temple of Pity, of its situation, construction, and groups of painting with which its walls were decorated, was borrowed from a poem, now lost, entitled *The Temple of Pity,* written by my brother while he and Collins were school-fellows at Winchester college." [15] Perhaps this cribbed temple of Pity helps explain why Joseph Warton and Collins did not, finally, publish their odes together.

The "Ode to Fear" is one of Collins' more striking poems. I have already, in the last chapter, discussed one passage from it, and that passage conveys the tone of the strophe and antistrophe. The verse is nervous, rapid, vivid, calling to the full upon the techniques of personification, but presenting these personified figures not in extended portraits but in flashing glimpses: "Whilst *Vengeance,* in the lurid air,/ Lifts her red Arm, expos'd and bare" (20-21). We are inclined to agree with the poet when he asks "Who, *Fear,* this ghastly Train can see,/ And look not madly wild, like Thee?" (24-25). The epode[16] celebrates Æschylus and Sophocles as those who could best invoke Fear, and concludes:

> O *Fear,* I know Thee by my throbbing Heart,
>   Thy with'ring Pow'r inspir'd each mournful Line,
> Tho' gentle *Pity* claim her mingled Part,
>   Yet all the Thunders of the Scene are thine!   (42-45)

In the antistrophe Collins gives us Fear in nature and in poetry; he asks "Be mine, to read the Visions old/ Which thy awak'ning Bards have told—(54-55). But he also asks "Ne'er be I found by thee o'erawed" at the fear of supernatural phenomena. The Fear he wishes to experience is the literary emotion, which, one cannot help guessing, may have been to Collins the genuine emotion. Hence he concludes with an invocation to Fear's greatest prophet, Shakespeare:

> O Thou whose Spirit most possest
> The sacred Seat of *Shakespeare*'s Breast!
> By all that from thy Prophet broke,

In thy Divine Emotions spoke:
Hither again thy Fury deal,
Teach me but once like Him to feel:
His *Cypress Wreath* my Meed decree,
And I, O *Fear,* will dwell with *Thee!*   (64-71)

The alert reader will catch both Miltonic and Shakespearian echoes, particularly in the antistrophe of "Ode to Fear." The ending, of course, is modelled after "L'Allegro" and "Il Penseroso." Of this ending Mrs. Barbauld complained: "The complimentary valediction so often imitated from MILTON, *And I, O Fear, will dwell with thee,* is in this instance but a compliment; for however a man might be content to have his days tinged with the soft influence of a penseroso-melancholy; he could not, for any reward, wish to subject himself habitually to the distracting emotions of such a passion as Fear." [17]

Scarcely any comment, it seems to me, could be more off the point, and I would not bother to quote it did it not give me the opportunity to say what I think the point is: Collins would subject himself *even* to Fear if she could teach him to feel like Shakespeare and thus provide for him the cypress-wreath—here not the emblem of death but the crown of the tragic poet—as his meed. We should remember, also, that if the 1705 translation of Aristotle which I quoted is any indication of the concept of tragic Fear held by Collins, this emotion would not have been a "distracting" one in the sense Mrs. Barbauld apparently means, though the lines of Collins' poem may explain in part the distraction which kept him from writing tragedies. We know that Collins was planning one or more tragedies which he never completed; they may have remained unfinished simply because no intelligent and self-critical young poet who could seriously write the conclusion of the "Ode to Fear" would be likely to be content with any tragedy he wrote.

In writing an "Ode to Simplicity," the next poem in the volume, Collins was running the danger of descending into cant. "Simplicity" had, by the 1740's, come to be a blanket term of praise which could mean everything or nothing.[18] It was an esthetic catchword of the time, and as such meant no more than our catchword "original." One who has read even casually very much of the esthetic

—and not only literary—criticism of the period will recognize the concepts in Collins' poem as those going the rounds at the time: the ideas that "nature" is essentially simple; that the Greeks, in imitating nature, had done so supremely because they captured her simplicity; that the Romans had violated the principle of simplicity and hence were, along with all succeeding artists, esthetically inferior to the Greeks. These are precisely the ideas one would expect to find in a poem on simplicity written in the 1740's.

Yet Collins writes a vital poem. The ideas may be dead to us; they may have been (though I think not) moribund at the time; but they were very alive to the young poet, and he manages to make them come alive in the ode. Collins considered Simplicity actively as a spiritual attribute underlying all creative activity. It was the voice of the young poetic rebel, for the call he makes is exactly that which lies behind every new movement in poetry: the call to return to nature.

> O THOU by *Nature* taught,
> To breathe her genuine Thought,
> In Numbers warmly pure, and sweetly strong   (1-3)

he begins, and makes "Fancy" her, or *Pleasure's* child. Disdaining the "wealth of art," she comes "with hermits heart" in "Attic Robe array'd." She it was who "Sooth'd sweetly sad *Electra's* Poet's Ear," by whom he means Sophocles. But when, in Greece "holy *Freedom* died/ No equal Haunt allur'd thy future Feet." He then asks, in stanza five:

> O Sister meek of Truth,
> To my admiring Youth,
> Thy sober Aid and native Charms infuse!
> The Flow'rs that sweetest breathe,
> Tho' Beauty cull'd the Wreath,
> Still ask thy Hand to range their order'd Hues.   (25-30)

Even in nature, Simplicity as a supernatural force creates beauty, and Collins asks that force to aid him in his own acts of creation. Simplicity is the principle of beauty. We today, I think, might speak of "Form" rather than Simplicity and come close to what Collins means.

[104]

In stanzas six and seven he traces the fate of Simplicity in Rome and later: "No more, in Hall or Bow'r/ The Passions own thy Pow'r . . ." (37-38). The implication at the end of stanza seven is that Simplicity cannot be induced to return as long as men servilely sing only of love.

Stanza eight marks the climax of the poem:

> Tho' Taste, tho' Genius bless,
> To some divine Excess,
> Faints the cold Work till Thou inspire the whole;
> What each, what all supply,
> May court, may charm our Eye,
> Thou, only Thou can'st raise the meeting Soul!   (43-48)

This final stanza is a perfect decrescendo. It is not Taste and Genius to which we must turn for great poetry, but rather to this supreme principle, Simplicity, from which the sons of Nature learn.

It is interesting that in the recently published *Drafts and Fragments* we have what is no doubt an early draft of this poem. The gross outline is the same, the meter is the same adaptation of Milton's "Nativity Ode," and some of the images are the same or very similar. This draft opens as an ode to Fancy rather than to Simplicity; and, if it were not for the title, I do not believe we would think of Simplicity as an attribute of Fancy except by implication through the fragmentary poem. It is possible that Collins realized before he had gone very far that his conception of Fancy, clear enough in the first stanza of the draft, would not carry what he wanted to say—was, in fact, only part of a larger conception. At any rate, he gave the draft the title "To Simplicity," adopted some of the ideas he had already worked out, and wrote another poem. Certainly the poem which appeared in the published volume of *Odes* is much better than we can imagine even the perfected draft would have been, although some of the stanzas of the draft have merit:

> O Chaste Unboastfull Guide
> O'er all my Heart preside
> And 'midst my Cave in breathing Marble wrought
> In sober Musing near

        With Attic Robe appear
        And charm my sight and prompt my temperate thought.
                                                    (31-36)

This is Simplicity (or is it Fancy?), and here there is not only the general invocation of Greece, but particularly of the "breathing marble" of Greek sculpture, the vision of which, as I have pointed out, seems to have influenced Collins' own imaginings of his personifications.

Pity, Fear, the principle of beauty summed up in Simplicity: all these poetic attributes culminate inevitably in the "Ode on the Poetical Character." Sir Edgerton Brydges remarked that this ode is "here and there a little involved and obscure," but he then says that "its general conception is magnificent." [19] Langhorne had said that "This ode is so infinitely abstracted and replete with high enthusiasm, that it will find few readers capable of entering into the spirit of it, or of relishing its beauties." [20] Robert Anderson said flatly that "His *Ode on the Poetical Character* is so extremely wild and extravagant, that it seems to have been written wholly during the tyranny of imagination. It is entirely abstracted, and, in some parts it may be thought blameably obscure; but there are some, however, whose congenial spirits may keep pace with him in his most eccentric flights; and from some of his casual strokes, may catch those sublime ideas which, like him, they have experienced, but have never been able to express." [21] I hope Dr. Anderson did not intend to say that Colllins himself was unsuccessful in expressing these sublime ideas; the modern reader may continue to think so.

For the "Ode on the Poetical Character" is penetrable, and it is possibly the poem which crystallizes an essence of Collins. Perhaps as well as any other poem it displays the characteristics which I have described as belonging to the Pindarick ode: it has as its subject an idea of high seriousness; it is rhapsodic in structure and employs vastly periodic sentences and sharp, surprising transitions; it invokes sublime objects—even the most sublime Object; it it consciously elevated in tone and language; and it makes full use of the possibilities of personified abstractions.

The whole twenty-two lines of the strophe is one sentence of the "As once . . . so thus . . ." construction; and, once the reader has spotted the "thus" in line seventeen, its meaning is not obscure, even though it does require us to remember for several lines what the poet has said. Collins calls upon his inaccurate memory of the story of Florimel, Amoret, and the tourney in Book IV Canto v of *The Faerie Queene* to provide him with the magic girdle, "The Cest of amplest Pow'r" of creativity which Fancy assigns to few "To gird their blest prophetic Loins,/ And gaze her Visions wild, and feel unmix'd her Flame!" (21-22).

The epode enters boldly upon the myth of the poetic girdle. It is, so far as I can discover, Collins' own conception, and shows the true mythopaeic genius. According to it, the weaving of the girdle of poetry is a product of the act of divine imagination by which the world was created:

> Long by the Lov'd *Enthusiast* woo'd,
> Himself in some Diviner Mood
> Retiring, sate with her alone,
> And plac'd her on his Saphire Throne . . .
> And Thou, Thou rich-hair'd Youth of Morn,
> And all thy subject Life was born!   (29-40)

This last couplet has caused some complaint, but it seems to me clear enough. If the ambiguities had been invented by a seventeenth- or twentieth-century poet, they would be much admired. The rich-haired youth is both Apollo as the sun and Apollo as the god of poetry; and his subject Life is both life subject to, dependent upon him as the sun, and the subject of his art. The act of poetic creation is thus doubly connected with God's act of creating the material universe. The epode concludes with the question,

> Where is the Bard, whose Soul can now
> Its high presuming Hopes avow?
> Where He who thinks, with Rapture blind,
> This hallow'd Work for Him design'd?   (51-54)

I think no artist has been called to a higher task than that which Collins has put upon the poet. The epode reflects the Platonic conception echoed in Spenser; it is implied that, besides Spenser, only Milton in England has fulfilled this calling. The antistrophe, full of verbal echoes of and direct references to Milton, is a paean to that poet. Milton is the archetype of the poetical character, the one who can best inspire the poet of succeeding ages; but also,

> My trembling Feet his guiding Steps pursue;
>   In vain—Such Bliss to One alone,
>   Of all the Sons of Soul was known,
>   And Heav'n, and *Fancy*, kindred Pow'rs,
>   Have now o'erturn'd th'inspiring Bow'rs,
> Or curtain'd close such Scene from ev'ry future View.
>   (71-76)

These lines express more than the protest against didactic poetry published by Joseph Warton in the Preface to his volume of odes. The poet despairs of any poet's ever again being able to hear the "ancient Trump" which inspired Milton.

Although the sense of the whole poem is clear enough, there are a few lines whose precise meaning eludes me. I do not find, for example, satisfactory antecedents for "its" and "his" in lines 61 and 62. This vague reference of pronominal adjectives is a failing to which Collins was subject; like most young poets, he expected his ideal reader to be a mind reader and to fathom what he meant despite obscurities. The obscurities, however, do not obscure the verbal beauty of the poem, or the genuine passion which it conveys. In "Ode on the Poetical Character" Collins came as close as he ever came, as close as anyone in the eighteenth century ever came, to writing successfully a sublime Pindarick. Perhaps he came as close as possible to writing a successful example of that *kind* of poem. Certainly no one until the nineteenth century came closer.

IV *The Patriotic Odes*

In the four odes I have just discussed, Collins makes a statement about the nature of poetry and the poet's task. The next four odes may be called "political" or "patriotic." They all have to do with the relation of man to his country. The first ode of this second group is the "Ode Written at the beginning of the Year 1746," more easily known as "How Sleep the Brave." It is Collins' perfect poem, the complete justification for his poetics. It is as fine a short poem as was written during the eighteenth century; I think there are not another twelve lines in English more nearly reaching Gre-

cian perfection. There are other poems as good—a few—but none
better, none more elegantly wrought, none more felicitous in expression.

One cannot analyze perfection any more than one could analyze a miracle, but one can talk about it.

> How sleep the Brave, who sink to Rest,
> By all their country's Wishes blest!
> When *Spring*, with dewy Fingers cold,
> Returns to deck their hallow'd Mold,
> She there shall dress a sweeter Sod,
> Than *Fancy's* Feet have ever trod.
>
> 2.
>
> By Fairy Hands their Knell is rung,
> By Forms unseen their Dirge is sung;
> There *Honour* comes, a Pilgrim grey,
> To bless the Turf that wraps their Clay,
> And *Freedom* shall a-while repair,
> To dwell a weeping Hermit there!

The poem was written no doubt in commemoration of the soldiers who fell in the Battle of Falkirk, January 17, 1746, when the
English were defeated by the troops of the Young Pretender. Or,
if Collins was reckoning by the Old Style, by which April was the
second month of the new year, it may have been written following
the Battle of Culloden on April 16, when the hopes of the Stuarts
were finally crushed.[22] The particular occasion does not matter;
the fact is clear that the poem is a tribute to soldiers who have
fallen in battle, and that Spring, the time of new life, comes to
dress their graves. The hint of personification is just enough, and
exactly right. "Dewy" is one of Collins' favorite words; it is used
no less than four times in the odes. But here, as with the other
words in the poem—we except one—we search in vain for any
epithet to surpass its very un-graveyard-like delicacy. "Dewy fingers cold" is all we need to know about this Spring. The implication of the poem is that these graves are beyond being hallowed
by mortal means. If there is a defect in the poem it is, to me,
"Fairy Hands." These are not quite the beings whom we should

want to deck our hallowed places, but "Forms unseen" is, again, right—suggestive of the supernatural without compelling us to visualize any of those beings traditionally supposed to haunt graves. Collins has succeeded in what, particularly in the 1740's with Young and Blair in the shrubbery, was the extremely difficult task of taking us out of the conventional poetic cemetery to a place of freshness and beauty.

Honour is a pilgrim from the real world which possesses now no such honor as these heroes displayed, grey not only by the tradition of pilgrims but also in contrast to the brightness of their renown, come to pay tribute to the shrine which gives him his being. The weeping hermit *Freedom* appropriately retires to this spot where those who died for him lie forever. There is the suggestion, by making Freedom a hermit, both that freedom itself is of the solitary mind and that only by pennance is it to be secured. The hermit is a recollection also of the Druidical hermits who were regarded both as poets and as fighters for freedom. The fact that Spring comes along with these figures is not merely a remark on the season but a symbolic representation of the hope that Freedom and Honour may arise from these graves like flowers if we but pay them heed. But we must not push an interpretation too far.

The "train" or series of personifications is a device Collins might have adopted from Milton, and there is something reminding us of the Minor Poems in the tone of Collins' piece. The Pilgrim grey may have been a recollection of "With Pilgrim steps in amice grey" from *Paradise Regained* (IV, 427). "Returns to deck their hallow'd mold" is very possibly Collins' remembrance of *Paradise Lost,* "Adam, earth's hallowed mould,/ Of God inspired . . ." (V, 321). But no matter how far we track suggestive sources, the poem is Collins' own, and his finest achievement.

It was an achievement for which he labored, and evidence of the labor is to be found in several stanzas of the "Ode, to a Lady on the Death of Colonel Ross in the Action of Fontenoy." "Colonel Ross" is an occasional poem, and we cannot feel that Collins was deeply stirred by the occasion. As we have noted, there is no reason to think he knew Ross well, if at all; and, although the Oxford edition of Collins perpetuates the story that the poem was addressed to a Miss Elizabeth Goddard (Joseph Warton mentions her in the "racetrack" letter to Thomas), no scholarship has definitely uncovered the existence of this young lady or succeeded in connecting her either with Collins or with Harting, Sussex, where she was supposed to have lived. This is not to say she did not exist; it is only to remark that, as we have seen, probably she did not play a much more important part in Collins' life than Ross himself, who could not have been very well known to Collins since the title of the poem promotes him from Captain to Colonel.[23] The poem, then, may be taken as a kind of exercise. Unfortunately, I must agree with most commentators that it is not an entirely successful exercise, its chief interest lying in the anticipations of "How Sleep the Brave," which are the best parts of the poem:

4.

Blest Youth, regardful of thy Doom,
Aërial Hands shall build thy Tomb,
 With shadowy Trophies crown'd:
Whilst *Honor* bath'd in Tears shall rove
To sigh thy Name thro' ev'ry Grove,
 And call his Heros round.

. . . .

7.

But lo where, sunk in deep Despair,
Her Garments torn, her Bosom bare,
 Impatient *Freedom* lies!
Her matted Tresses madly spread,
To ev'ry Sod, which wraps the Dead,
 She turns her joyless Eyes.

Freedom reminds us of a Delacroix painting. I find her just a little too disheveled to be convincing. Both these stanzas were omitted from Collins' last revision of the poem, published in Dodsley's *Collection* in 1748. For stanza four is subsituted:

O'er him whose doom thy virtues grieve
Aerial forms shall sit at eve
 And bend the pensive head!

And, fall'n to save his injur'd land,
Imperial Honour's awful hand
Shall point his lonely bed!

This is something of an improvement, though not so great a one as we should like. Since it moves closer both to "How Sleep the Brave" and "Ode to Evening," it suggests that Collins recognized his own best strain.

Stanza eight in the 1746 version is possibly the worst thing Collins ever wrote from a purely verbal standpoint, particularly the last three lines:

Till *William* seek the sad Retreat,
And bleeding at her sacred Feet
Present the sated Sword.

The repetition of the "ee" and "s" sounds reminds one of "a brazen canstick turn'd"; if Gray's eye lit first on these lines when he opened Collins' volume, we can understand his remarking on a "bad ear." We note happily that Collins also omitted this stanza from his 1748 revision, which is, all and all, a considerably better poem than he had at first published. But I wish I could be sure that the omission of this stanza were clearly owing to the dictates of Collins' critical faculties. The William referred to is no doubt William, Duke of Cumberland, who led the English to victory in 1745. He had been much adulated, and there was general hope that he would display magnanimity in victory, as we see by the fact that it is to Freedom that he is to "present the sated sword." However, as Lecky says, "The Hanoverian army, and the Duke of Cumberland who commanded it, displayed in their triumph a barbarity which recalled the memory of Sedgemoor and of the Bloody Assize, while the courage, the loyalty, and the touching fidelity of the Highlanders to their fallen chief cast a halo of romantic interest around his cause." [24] It is depressingly possible that, by removing the stanza, Collins merely wanted to remove a flattering reference to Cumberland.

If the "Ode to Mercy" was also written early enough in 1746, it may be another, but less direct, reference to Cumberland. This poem is one of the most consistent personifications which Collins wrote. "Mercy," as an "allegoric description" doesn't do enough to

make an allegory, yet she is a well-visualized figure. She is not,
however, enough to make the ode to her a very exciting poem. It
is a poem which has merit, but not great merit. Indeed, its greatest merit may be its very unpretentiousness. With this short ode
may also be discussed the "Ode to Peace," which follows "Ode
to Evening," and shares with "Mercy" the unpretentiousness, but
which has even less merit. The stanza form is the same as in
"Colonel Ross," a metrical inversion of the form derived from Milton which Collins used in "Simplicity." He does not seem happy in
the stanza, and—the worst thing which could happen in an "alle-
goric-descriptive" poem—his powers of visualizing his personification seem to fail him. The picture is not clear, or, if it is clear, it
is ludicrous. I do not fully understand, much less see, the first
stanza:

> O THOU, who bad'st thy Turtles bear
> Swift from his Grasp thy golden Hair,
>   And sought'st thy native Skies:
> When *War*, by Vultures drawn from far,
> To *Britain* bent his Iron Car,
>   And bad his Storms arise!

So far as I can tell, what is happening is that War, in an iron car
drawn by vultures, has been trying to catch hold of Peace's golden
hair, but is interrupted in this playfulness when Peace tells her
turtledoves to snatch it away from him. Or perhaps he already
had her hair in his grasp? I do not know, and I must say the poem
does not make me care. Similarly the third stanza is confusing:

> O *Peace*, thy injur'd Robes up-bind,
> O rise, and leave not one behind
>   Of all thy beamy Train:
> The *British* Lion, Goddess sweet,
> Lies stretch'd on Earth to kiss thy Feet,
>   And own thy holier Reign.   (13-18)

I do not know who the beamy train is; there is no indication of
any such followers in stanza two. The colon (Is this an example of
bad punctuation; is Collins responsible for the colon, or is his
printer? I wish we knew.)—the colon makes us think it may be

the British Lion, however unlikely it is that he should be "beamy"; but, if he is in her train, what is he doing at her feet? And where is Peace going when she rises? To England, presumably. But then where have we been all this time? This is Collins at his very worst, and is the sort of thing which, taken as typical, can make a laughing-stock of eighteenth-century poetry.

The poem ends with the union of *Peace* and *Honour*—a laudable though scarcely original sentiment. But then the poem is, as I said, a modest one, both in scope and in pretension (for Collins is not attempting here to be, if I may say so, more than *slightly* sublime). And, in view of his greater odes, the failure of this one need not disconcert us—for that it is a failure I need not pretend to doubt.

The "Ode to Liberty" which follows "Mercy" in Collins' arrangement, is the longest poem in the volume. Rich in allusion and dense in texture, it brings together in the second epode the leading ideas of all the poems we have considered up to this point. It is another progress piece, this time tracing the progress of Liberty from ancient Greece to eighteenth-century England.

The first sentence of the strophe needs some explication, but once we see that the object of "to view" is "Locks" we can understand that *Freedom* loved to see these because it meant that the Spartan youths were going into battle for her honor. The legend is that, before the battle of Thermopylae, the Persian scouts were astonished to see the valorous, dangerous Spartans gaily combing their long hair, as was their custom before an engagement. The next sentence refers to the story of two Greek youths, Harmodius and Aristogeiton, who took the occasion of a festival in honor of Athene, Goddess of Wisdom, when their going armed would not be noted, to strike down Hipparchon the usurper.[25] The "she" in the next to the last line quoted refers to Wisdom, and "her prompted wound" in the last line of the sentence must mean "the wound which Wisdom prompted":

> WHO shall awake the *Spartan* Fife,
> And call in solemn Sounds to Life,
> The Youths, whose Locks divinely spreading,
>   Like vernal Hyacinths in sullen Hue,
> At once the Breath of Fear and Virtue shedding,
>   Applauding *Freedom* lov'd of old to view?

> What New *Alcæus*, Fancy-blest,
> Shall sing the Sword, in Myrtles drest,
>   At *Wisdom*'s Shrine a-while its Flame concealing,
>   (What Place so fit to seal a Deed renown'd?)
>   Till she her brightest Lightnings round revealing,
>   It leap'd in Glory forth, and dealt her prompted Wound!
>   (1-12)

The rest of the strophe imposes no particular difficulties, and has one of Collins' most striking images:

> No, *Freedom*, no, I will not tell,
>   How *Rome*, before thy weeping Face,
> With heaviest Sound, a Giant-statue, fell,
>   Push'd by a wild and artless Race,
>   From off its wide ambitious Base,
> When Time his Northern Sons of Spoil awoke,
>   And all the blended Work of Strength and Grace,
>   With many a rude repeated Stroke,
> And many a barb'rous Yell, to thousand Fragments broke.
>   (17-25)

The "Giant-statue" can be taken, as Mr. Ainsworth suggests, as "in a somewhat Platonic sense a Divine Idea or pattern of Liberty shadowed forth in earthly form." [26] Collins develops this concept at the end of the poem, and it is perfectly in accord with the interest he often displayed in classical sculpture, with which he seems to have associated Platonic Ideas.

The pattern of the epode is determined by the first lines: "Yet ev'n, where'er the least appear'd,/ Th'admiring World thy Hand rever'd" (26-27). "The least" refers to the least fragment of the statue. Wherever such a part survived in the former Roman world, the inhabitants were able dimly to perceive the divine form of the whole. Thus Liberty did not wholly perish in Florence, Pisa, Venice, Switzerland. At the end of the epode the poet invokes the presence of Liberty in England:

> The Magic works, Thou feel'st the Strains,
> One holier Name alone remains;
> The perfect Spell shall then avail,
> Hail Nymph, ador'd by *Britain,* Hail!   (60-63)

The antistrophe, part of which I quoted in the last chapter, celebrates the "blessed divorce" of the British Isles from France, and the establishment of Liberty in England; and, in the second epode, Collins proceeds to trace her history there. This is the climax of the poem, and it is worth noticing immediately that one of the symbols which Collins is at pains to establish in the first few lines is that of the Druids. I will return to the Druids in discussing the "Ode Occasion'd by the Death of Mr. Thomson," but I must anticipate my remarks in that discussion by pointing out that in the "mythology" of the mid-eighteenth century the Druids had a special place,[27] for the Druid was thought to be a poet-priest of nature, fabled for his supposed resistance to the Roman invaders, hence an appropriate symbol of British freedom, and at the same time a bard who by his poems inspired the early Britons to great feats of bravery. The second epode opens with the Druid shrine:

> Then too, 'tis said, an hoary Pile,
> 'Midst the green Navel of our Isle,
> Thy Shrine in some religious Wood,
> O Soul-enforcing Goddess stood!
> There oft the painted Native's Feet,
> Were wont thy Form celestial meet:
>
> . . . .
>
> Yet still, if Truth those Beams infuse,
> Which guide at once, and charm the Muse,
> Beyond yon braided Clouds that lie,
> Paving the light-embroider'd Sky:
> Amidst the bright pavilion'd Plains,
> The beauteous *Model* still remains.
> There happier than in Islands blest,
> Or Bow'rs by Spring or *Hebe* drest,
> The Chiefs who fill our *Albion*'s Story,
> In warlike Weeds, retir'd in Glory,
> Hear their consorted *Druids* sing
> Their Triumphs to th'immortal String.   (89-112)

The Platonic "beauteous Model" has already been prepared for in the statue of Rome. Here it ties the history of Freedom in the Ancient world with the Druids in Britain. We see this concept developed in the next lines, where Collins asks:

> How may the Poet now unfold
> What never Tongue or Numbers told?
> How learn delighted, and amaz'd,
> What Hands unknown that Fabric rais'd?
> Ev'n now before his favor'd Eyes,
> In *Gothic* Pride it seems to rise!
> Yet *Græcia's* graceful Orders join,
> Majestic thro' the mix'd Design;   (113-120)

The " Gothic Pride" and "Græcia's orders" bring together the ideas of poetry and liberty in architectural guise—the form in which, according to Palladian concepts, the most perfect expression of orderly beauty was possible. Keeping in mind the vague eighteenth-century use of the word "Gothic" to indicate anything mediaeval, we have already seen the "Gothic" background for Liberty in the Druids; we must remember also Collins' own interest, and that of the Wartons and presumably other of their friends, in the earlier English literature. Writers as late as Spenser were called "Gothic." It is probable that to Collins and Warton the word still had vaguely pejorative force; but, in so far as the "Gothic" Druids could represent an epoch of freedom and poetry, the word is commendatory. To the Gothic Pride, however, is to be joined the corrective purity and discipline of Greece—perfectly appropriate in terms of the strophe of this poem and in terms of common conceptions of the values of Greek art. The "Platonic idea" of Liberty is Greek; so are the neoclassic ideals of poetry, and these latter, it is implied, can be achieved only where the former are in force.

There has been much complaint about the last eight lines of the poem:

> Her let our Sires and Matrons hoar
> Welcome to *Britain's* ravag'd Shore,
> Our Youths, enamour'd of the Fair,
> Play with the Tangles of her Hair,
> Till in one loud applauding Sound,
> The Nations shout to Her around,
> O how supremely art thou blest,
> Thou, Lady, Thou shalt rule the West!   (137-144)

Most commentators have objected that, in the words of J. M. Murry, "To apply to Liberty, the Lady who shall rule the West, the phrase which Milton used of those who preferred the company of Amaryllis and Neæra to the last infirmity of a noble mind. *Curiosa infelicitas!*" [28] The phrase can be defended as appropriate. The Sires and Matrons hoar have in Milton's time achieved this liberty; now it is possible for the youths to need no further spur to fame, and they may indeed "sport with Amaryllis in the shade" with no need "To scorn delights, and live laborious days" or perhaps not even strictly to "meditate the thankless Muse," since in the presence of Liberty, and only in her presence, is great artistic achievement possible. The allusion to Milton is to that part of *Lycidas* dealing with the poet and his thirst for fame; Collins subtly reverses the meaning of the Miltonic passage, but in doing so he reinforces the ideas introduced by the figure of the Druids earlier in the second epode: the idea that liberty and artistic achievement go hand in hand.

Mr. Ainsworth has dealt thoroughly with Spenserian and Miltonic influences on this poem, and I see no need to recapitulate his work. He also deals at length with the relation of Collins' poem to Thomson's *Liberty*, a connection perfectly likely in view of the friendship between the two poets, though I should think Collins might have absorbed the other's ideas in conversation rather than by reading through his very long and tiresome poem. The resemblances of thought and structure between the two poems are sufficiently close to compel belief that Thomson's ideas were the principal source for his young friend's, but the verbal parallels which Mr. Ainsworth cites do not force me to say that Collins had studied Thomson's poem very closely. [29]

The "Ode to Liberty" is certainly a major poem of the 1740's. There is a perceptibly sustained intellectual effort behind it which none of Collins' other poems displays quite so clearly, and this intellectual effort is for the most part effectively embodied in the texture of the poetry. One does not have the feeling here—as I do in "Peace" and "Colonel Ross" at least— that Collins set out to dress up some more or less coherent thoughts in poetic form, but rather that the ideas and the poetry are co-animate and in essence inseparable. Without Collins' way of putting them, we do not have Collins' exact ideas. Yet despite what analysis reveals in the poem, I am left vaguely dissatisfied with it. The source of this dissatisfaction may, however, be a back-handed compliment to Collins, for it springs somehow from the fact that the poem seems to me, as it has to others, so strangely to foreshadow Shelley and Coleridge on the same themes.[30] This is not a very high compliment for so good a poem; I have, indeed, already paid it a better one, and what I have just said should certainly not be taken as implying that the "Ode to Liberty" is not worth reading for its own sake.

V *"Ode to Evening"*

The most famous poem in the volume of *Odes on Several Descriptive and Allegoric Subjects* is "Ode to Evening," which with "How Sleep the Brave" is Collins' undisputed contribution to that small body of English lyrics which posterity has agreed to keep immortal. The poem has evoked a perennial fascination, and particularly within the last few decades a considerable body of criticism has grown up around it—a testimonial to its merit, though hardly the best testimonial. Perhaps the best testimonial is the simple fact that, with Gray's "Elegy," it is virtually the only poem from the mid-eighteenth century of which every reader knows at least the title.

I am willing to fly in the teeth of most twentieth-century criticism and say that "Ode to Evening" is essentially a simple poem, that its great values are mostly on the surface, and that these are great values because they are on the surface, where Collins intended them to be. The poem is both painterly and musical—the sights and sounds of evening are evoked, and it is the evocation which makes the poem approach greatness. That Collins may have intended what he says about Evening personified to bear some relation to the ideas in the rest of the odes that we have discussed is perfectly possible, though I am not convinced such is the case; but, if it is the case, it still has no bearing whatsoever on what seem to me the values of the poem. I think we may dismiss quite lightly these sub-surface meanings: if they had been really important to Collins, he would have insisted upon them more pointedly and in the manner we find in the other poems; for Col-

lins was, we must never forget, a mid-eighteenth-century poet and
therefore intended his verse to mean what it seemed to mean, not
what it seems to us to mean.

The meaning of the first forty lines at least is plain enough. In
the first twenty lines the poet asks Evening to teach him

> To breathe some soften'd Strain,
> Whose Numbers stealing thro' thy darkening Vale,
> May not unseemly with its Stillness suit (16-18)

—the kind of poetry in accord with this particular aspect of Nature. Does "Evening" by synecdoche stand for "Nature"? Commentators have not infrequently suggested the possibility, and I
will not object so long as it is made plain that this is not yet
Wordsworth's Nature; and, if it is not Wordsworth's Nature, there
is little point in insisting on the synecdoche. That Collins' intentions here do not really anticipate the Romantics is sufficiently
indicated by one of the poems in *Drafts and Fragments,* which
bears a clear relationship to "Ode to Evening." It is number three
in the volume,[31] and begins in the first four stanzas with an invocation to the urban genii:

> Take all that to the silent Sod
> Prefer the sounding street
> And Let your echoing squares be trod
> By their unresting feet. (13-16)

The only hint of Wordsworthism in these first sixteen lines occurs in stanza three, where the poet suggests to the city genii that
they:

> Take Them who know not how to prize
> The Walks to Wisdom dear
> The Gradual Fruits and varying skies
> That point the gradual Year. (9-12)

"The Walks to Wisdom dear" sounds like a hint of Wordsworth;
but, if it is such a hint, it is not one which Collins develops. For
there is no where else any intimation that the poet expects from

Nature any power more deeply interfused. On the contrary, Collins says,

> Let me where'er wild Nature leads
> My sight Enamour'd look
> And chuse my hymning Pipe from Reeds
> That roughen oer the Brook
>
> Some time when Morning oer [the] Plain
> Her radiant Mantle throws
> I'll mark the Clouds where sweet Lorrain
> His orient Colours chose   (21-28)

And at noontime he will seek the cheerful lime trees which Ruysdael drew, and

> Then on some Heath all wild and bare
> With more delight I[']ll stand
> Than He who sees with wondring air
> The Works of Rosa's hand
>
> There where some Rocks deep Cavern gapes
> Or in some tawny dell
> I'll seem to see the Wizzard Shapes
> That from his Pencill fell
>
> But when Soft Evening o'er the Plain
> Her gleamy Mantle throws
> I'll mark the Clouds whence sweet Lorraine
> His   colour chose   (33-44)

The next three stanzas are so fragmentary as to make any but highly speculative interpretation impossible, but the last two stanzas make the meaning plain. He is speaking of the moon:

> What Art can paint the modest ray
> So sober chaste and cool
> As round yon Cliffs it seems to play
> Or skirts yon glimmering Pool?
>
> The tender gleam her Orb affords
> No Poet can declare

Altho' he chuse the softest words
That e'er were sigh'd in air.   (57-64)

It is not in what Nature can do to his soul that Collins is interested, but in what she can do for his art, and it is to be noticed that Collins looks at the landscape in terms of the works of painters. His concern, as explicitly stated in this fragmentary draft and as we now understand him to have said quite clearly in the first twenty lines of "Ode to Evening," is the very neoclassical one of imitating nature. The word "Nature" is no doubt to be taken in a more "romantic" sense than Pope would have understood it, but Pope would have understood exactly the drift of Collins' poem. Collins confined the meaning of "Nature" somewhat more closely to the rocks and rills we think of when we hear the word rather than to "The nature of things" which the Augustans loosely meant by the term; but what Collins wants to do with his "Nature" is quite thoroughly Augustan.

The next twenty lines of "Ode to Evening" again present no difficulties. Evening is the time of mystery, which for Collins is embodied in the Hours and Elves and Nymphs. It is also the time for "Pensive Pleasures sweet" who prepare Evening's car. This is the time of day when the poet asks, "Then let me rove some wild and heathy Scene," or, in the 1748 version of the poem, "Then lead, calm Vot'ress, where some sheety lake. . . ." I will briefly discuss this changed eighth stanza in a moment, but, so far as the meaning of the poem is concerned, it is of only minor significance. The point is that at this time of day the poet must observe nature (not become one with her—there is no hint of that idea) if he is going to breathe the softened strain: ". . . be mine the Hut,/ That . . .

marks o'er all
Thy Dewy Fingers draw
The gradual dusky Veil

—not for his soul, but for his art.

The last twelve lines sum up. In all four seasons—"while Spring . . . ," "while Summer . . ." and so on (and here I think only the 1748 version makes clear sense):

[122]

> So long sure-found beneath the Sylvan shed
> Shall Fancy, Friendship, Science, rose-lip'd Health
>   Thy gentlest Influence own,
>   And hymn thy fav'rite Name.   (49-52)

The "sylvan shed" is presumably the hut in line 34, and I used to wish we did not have to share this modest enclosure with "rose-lip'd Health" and her friends, who, if I come upon them suddenly, can still jar me as though I had encountered a sewing-circle busily at work in the Elysian Fields. It is, as a matter of fact, a high compliment to the timelessness of Collins' art that, when he does introduce something purely and simply of his own time, it stands out with such savage clarity. However, I did not say that "Ode to Evening" was perfect; the poetic fault, for many of us, lies in its conclusion. But though we may feel these personages introduced so suddenly in the last stanza to be out of place, it is clear enough that Collins' contemporaries did not find them in the least incongruous, and they do not obscure the meaning of the poem. They may enhance it, indeed. Up to line forty the poet has been concerned with his own art; now in the quiet and benevolent influence of evening not only art but also Fancy (the muse commonly invoked, incidentally, in Miltonic imitations), Friendship, and so on will through his poems "hymn thy fav'rite Name." The "fav'rite Name" is not revealed, and it is only at this point that we may allow ourselves to wonder if it may be "Nature." We do not know, for suddenly the essential subjectivity of the poem emerges. The "fav'rite Name" must ultimately be whatever name each of us chooses.

So far as the allegorical personages in line fifty are concerned, it seems to me possible that Collins sensed the necessity for the same sort of poetic daring which required Keats in the last stanza of "Ode to a Nightingale" to bring us back to apprehension of the ordinary world. Collins is not up to "Fled is that music:—Do I wake or sleep?", but ". . . hymn thy fav'rite Name" performs the same function in "Ode to Evening." It is a resolution of the chord, and in this world, not in some other: for "Fancy, Friendship, Science, rose-lip'd Health" were, we must remember, beings capable of assuming a reality for Collins' audience, and it is surely because of this fact that Collins substituted "rose-lip'd Health" for "smiling

Peace." With the substitution, the four figures become a series progressively more mundane and concrete (if one may suppose a concrete abstraction!). In becoming more concrete the train of personifications also moves from a general human attribute—or, at least, an attribute of poets—"Fancy," the imaginative and inventive faculty; through Friendship, a quality shared within a small group or even limited to two people; to Science (that is, "knowledge"), the pursuit of which, though it may be a joint venture, is ultimately a private affair; and finally to Health, which is purely the concern of one individual (and which, we might remember, Collins in 1748 may already have begun to worry about). Thus the whole range of important human activity and concern is summarized in these personifications, all of them owning the influence of the Goddess Evening, and all of them joining with the poet in his tribute to her.

And we must not forget that Evening here is a Goddess, a personification, Collins' most successful one. She approaches more nearly to an allegorical figure in the Spenserian sense than any other of Collins' creations; and, although the poetics of the poem is more Miltonic than Spenserian, Collins is able to use his personification in a way more Spenserian than Miltonic in that she is a medium through which vivid sensual imagery is made to emerge. It is the sensual qualities of the poem which are most amazing and which, as I have already insisted, make it approach greatness. These qualities cannot, naturally, be separated from the technique of the verse.

The stanza form is one which, so far as I know, was first used in English by Milton in his translation of Horace's *Ad Pyrrham:*

> What slender Youth bedew'd with liquid Odours
> Courts thee on Roses in some pleasant Cave,
> *Pyrrha* for whom bind'st thou
> In wreaths thy golden Hair . . .

Milton does not maintain this delicacy of verse through the next three stanzas of his translation, but the stanza quoted could be inspiration enough for any poet, though it was not enough to enliven much the elder Thomas Warton's "Ode to Taste." Joseph Warton was more successful when he too used the stanza in a translation of Horace's Ode XIII, Book III; but only Collins, of all those who have used it,[32] has made it the medium for a poem within the still living corpus of English lyrics. The actual stanza form, however, is not important except in so far as we must note that what has proved generally disadvantageous to other poets Collins makes his poem's greatest triumph: I mean the absence of rhyme. We are never aware when we read "Ode to Evening" that we are reading a blank lyric, a very rare form in English, and this is because Collins has with such utter mastery controlled the sound-values of his lines. In order to see Collins consciously working at his sounds, we can observe the changes made in the first few lines. Here is the 1746 version, followed by the revision printed by Dodsley in 1748:

> 1746:　IF sought of Oaten Stop, or Pastoral Song,
> 　　　　May hope, O pensive *Eve*, to sooth thine Ear
> 　　　　　Like thy own brawling Springs,
> 　　　　　Thy Springs, and dying Gales . . .

> 1748:　IF ought of Oaten Stop, or Pastoral Song
> 　　　　May hope, chaste *Eve*, to sooth thy modest Ear,
> 　　　　　Like thy own solemn Springs,
> 　　　　　Thy Springs, and dying Gales . . .

The change of three words is extremely interesting. It hardly needs to be pointed out that in the first line the repeated "o" sounds give, and must surely be intended to give, the sound of woodwinds, of an "oaten stop." It is easy to see that by changing "thine" to "thy modest" we add an additional accented "o" sound. The change from "brawling" to "solemn" does not so much change the vowel sound (though it improves the sense), but it helps us to see that all the changes move in the same direction. Chastity, modesty, and solemnity are qualities which we associate with a Goddess; that is, there is what one might call a religious overtone to all of the changes which fits in very well with and helps to reinforce the incidental religious images of "Pilgrim" in the fourteenth line, of "Vot'ress" introduced in the revised version in line twenty-nine, and of "hymn" introduced in the last line. I cannot insist very strongly on these religious overtones of the poem because, after all, in his revision Collins did eliminate "religious

Gleams" in line thirty-two (though introducing "Vot'ress"), and I do not believe we are justified in making them central in any interpretation of the poem. The religious aura is there to add to the general tone of quiet, contemplative solemnity which the poem evokes.

But the three changes in the first stanza do something else for the sound. Without losing the sibilant in "pensive," Collins adds two more in "modest" and "solemn." I cannot see that these are onomatopoetic in the way the "o" sounds are, but it is hardly an accident that there are eighteen sibilants in the first six lines, nine of them accented, while we must count another ten lines to find eighteen sibilants, and of these only four are accented. Collins is, to be short, using every device of assonance, alliteration, and internal rhyme to bind his poem into a unit of sound as well as one of meaning. Close examination reveals these subtle sound-links throughout the poem.

The senses of sight and sound are intermeshed. To me, lines five to eight convey a vivid visual image, which immediately shifts to the aural one of the hushed air and "short shrill Shriek" of the bat and sound of the beetle. Lines twenty-one to twenty-nine, beginning "for when thy folding Star arising shews," are abstract, though even we have here the "fresh'ning Dew." But immediately following these lines we come upon one of the most striking images in the poem. The change from the 1746 to the 1748 version is a triumph of taste:

> 1746:   Then let me rove some wild and heathy Scene,
> Or find some Ruin 'midst its dreary Dells,
> Whose Walls more awful nod
> By thy religious Gleams.

> 1748:   Then lead, calm Vot'ress, where some sheety lake
> Cheers the lone heath, or some time-hallow'd pile,
> Or up-land fallows grey
> Reflects it's last cool gleam.

The "Gothic" element in the first version—implied by "wild," "Ruin," "dreary," "awful," "religious"—was a fashionable affectation in the 1740's, and Collins clearly had the taste to see that it had nothing to do with the permanent significance of his poem. It was not Salvatore Rosa but Claude Lorrain who was appropriate to his theme. In the second version we have only a "time-hallow'd pile," which certainly might be "Gothic" but is not necessarily so. The second version also seems to me to be more concretely visual, and I must say I do not find in it the difficulties some others have discerned.[33] The "Vot'ress" seems a perfect epithet for Evening, and I have no difficulty in visualizing a heath, a calm lake reflecting the last rays of the sun glimmeringly upon the walls of the "time-hallow'd pile" and the "fallow uplands" at the edge of the lake upon which the pile rests. The revision is also an improvement in eliminating "nod," which, applied to walls, is disturbing.

Lines thirty-five to forty are a masterstroke:

> . . . be mine the Hut,
> That from the Mountain's Side,
> Views Wilds, and swelling Floods,
> And Hamlets brown, and dim-discover'd Spires,
> And hears their simple Bell, and marks o'er all
> Thy Dewy Fingers draw
> The gradual dusky Veil.

The senses are here combined; we feel our eyes straining through the dusk to make out the church spires from which the bell sounds, and sense the cool dews of the "gradual dusky Veil" as the whole scene fades into night.

This last effect, and indeed that of the lake and "time-hallow'd pile" as well, are ones which may well have been suggested to Collins by the paintings of Claude Lorrain, in whom, as we have seen from the verses quoted from *Drafts and Fragments,* Collins was interested. How informed this interest was, what opportunity actually to see a Claude painting Collins had, I do not know. I am not sure he would have ever had a chance to see works by any of the artists he mentioned, though I cannot, of course, say definitely. I suspect, however, that the references to Claude, Rosa, and Ruysdael are prompted as much by their reputations and by literature as by any very intimate exposure to their works. The comments have the patness of someone repeating what he has overheard in an outer room.

The "Ode to Evening" is, with "How Sleep the Brave," the triumph of Collins' poetry. In it we find fully applied the poetical theories he has stated or implied in the other odes—it is a perfect expression of the supreme quality of simplicity, of form; and it is because of this characteristic that I have said that the values of the poem are on the surface. They are on the surface in the same way that the values of Greek sculpture are. Penetrating into the marble will not make the Olympian Apollo a better statue; I do not believe that penetrating into "Ode to Evening" helps make it a better poem. In the last analysis, the poem is inexplicable; for, as nearly as any other poem, it embodies some of the qualities of Milton as praised in "Ode on the Poetical Character"; we do suddenly see in Collins the divine creator. Most remarkable of all, however, and quite unprepared for by the other poems, is the way Collins here breaks through the encircling walls of perceptions literary in origin into a world which he creates through his own senses and intelligence.

VI *The Manners and The Passions*

"Ode to Evening" is followed in the volume of odes by "Ode to Peace," which I have discussed, and this is followed by "The Manners. An Ode." Everyone who has studied Collins has agreed that this poem must have been the earliest written in the 1746 volume, and that it probably somehow reflects his decision to throw up his Demyship at Magdalen College and go to London. There is only internal evidence for this supposition, but the evidence is fairly strong. Since the poem may be the only one which directly reflects Collins' biography, I wish we knew more about the circumstances of its composition; but, as a matter of fact, we know only what the poem says; and whatever it says, if it says anything at all, about Collins' biography is not easy to get at.

What it very clearly says is that the poet is giving up books for "Nature" (and this is very clearly Pope's nature, not Wordsworth's); that he is leaving "the Porch, whose Roof is seen / Arch'd with th'enlivening Olive's Green"—that is, formal academic study —for "Life." These are the sort of sentiments one expects of young men at the university, and it would have surprised us only if Collins had not felt them. The purpose of this excursion from academe is also about what we would expect. He asks *Observance* (who is not very happily introduced and not at all visualized):

> To me in Converse sweet impart,
> To read in Man the native Heart,
> To learn, where Science sure is found,
> From Nature as she lives around:
> And gazing oft her Mirrour true
> By turns each shifting Image view!   (25-30)

—a perfectly safe neoclassical activity. Equally neoclassical is the expectation that

> Retiring hence to thoughtful Cell,
> As *Fancy* breathes her potent Spell,
> Not vain she finds the charmful Task,
> In Pageant quaint, in motley Mask,
> Behold before her musing Eyes,
> The countless *Manners* round her rise . . .   (37-42)

He also asks of *Humour:*

> Me too amidst thy Band admit,
> There where the young-eyed healthful *Wit,*
> (Whose Jewels in his crisped Hair
> Are plac'd each other's Beams to share,
> Whom no Delights from Thee divide)
> In Laughter loos'd attends thy Side!   (53-58)

We could wish that someone had preserved for us the diverting observations which Ragsdale says Collins made upon the characters from the greenroom at Drury Lane. At the conclusion of the poem Collins asks:

> O Nature boon, from whom proceed
> Each forceful Thought, each prompted Deed;
> If but from Thee I hope to feel,
> On all my Heart imprint thy Seal!
> Let some retreating Cynic find,
> Those oft-turn'd Scrolls I leave behind,
> The *Sports* and I this Hour agree,
> To rove thy Scene-full World with Thee!   (71-78)

We remember that Collins once before, in the "Ode to Fear," has asked, speaking of Shakespeare, "Teach me but once like him to feel." Here he asks again of Nature, "If but from thee I hope to feel. . . ." Did Collins believe himself deficient in emotion? We will return to this question later, but here we should note that it is from the "nature" of Pope—"the nature of things"—that he hopes to learn this lesson. There is not the slightest hint of the "romantic" in the poem.

"The Manners" is good-natured, and just good enough to make us wish Collins had done other things in this lighter vein. The sprightly octosyllabic couplets carry us along, and there is a play of wit which the other poems do not display. It is not Collins' best vein, but it is handled well enough to make us think that he never really found the style that could have been his own.

The last poem in the volume, in the place of honor, is "The Passions. An Ode for Music." By its title we should expect it to be paired with "The Manners," and to a small extent the expectation is justified. The pairing of the two poems seems on the surface to extend no further than the titles, and this being the case I hesitate to attempt, by forcing them into a preconceived context, to impose a unity which the volume only by implication displays. Yet there is every evidence, as we have seen, that Collins' primary interests were artistic—of the twelve poems, seven are quite explicitly concerned with art—and, this being the case, it can hardly be accidental that the final two poems are about the ingredients of art. The first deals with a relationship between the artist and "nature"; the second, with the relation of the artist to art itself. The poems are complementary rather than contrasting; and, if we look at them in this light, the pairing does make sense—provided, I must insist, that we do not press them too vigorously into an *a priori* scheme.

The very structure of "The Passions" discourages *a priori* schemata, for the ode is the only one of Collins' poems which follows Cowley in Pindarick irregularity. It opens with sixteen lines in tetrameter couplets and closes with a twenty-four line passage in the same measure, but between these sections are seventy-eight lines which are extremely irregular. This central passage opens with three tetrameter stanzas in ballad-rhyme, but after these twelve lines there is no discernible pattern either in metrics or rhyme. This is not to say that the section is disorderly. On the contrary, I believe it to be perhaps the finest display of Collins' technical skills, for it is, in effect, *durchkomponiert;* the rhythmic patterns and the rhymes are more fully expressive in themselves than in any other of Collins' poems.

The poem opens with a passage describing its occasion:

> When Music, Heav'nly Maid, was young,
> While yet in early *Greece* she sung,
> The Passions oft to hear her Shell,
> Throng'd around her magic Cell . . . (1-4)

until on one occasion "when all were fired, / Fill'd with Fury, rapt, inspir'd," and Madness rules the hour, each snatched an instrument and played. At this point we leave the tetrameter couplets and move into the long irregular section, opening with the three stanzas in alternate rhyme describing the efforts of Fear, Anger, and Despair; but then, with a linking-rhyme to Despair's stanza, Hope takes the lyre, and her performance is described in ten lines of exquisite variety introducing trochaic rhythms and pentameter lines among the prevailing iambic tetrameter, and concluding with a pair of Alexandrines, the second of which again creates a rhyme-link with the stanza on Despair. The metrical variations are used to emphasize the sense, as are the rhyme patterns:

> Still would Her Touch the Strain prolong,
>> And from the Rocks, the Woods, the Vale,
> She call'd on Echo still thro' all the Song;
>> And, where Her sweetest Theme She chose,
>> A soft responsive Voice was heard at ev'ry Close,
> And *Hope* enchanted smil'd, and wav'd Her golden Hair.
> And longer had She sung,—but with a Frown,
>> *Revenge* impatient rose,
> He threw his blood-stain'd Sword in Thunder down,
>> And with a with'ring Look,
>> The War-denouncing Trumpet took,
> And blew a Blast so loud and dread,
> Were ne'er Prophetic Sounds so full of Woe. (33-45)

"Woe," subtly, never finds a correspondent rhyme and is suspended in our ears like a single trumpet blast.

It seems clear that, what Collins does in this "irregular" section, he does only after the most careful consideration of the effect he wishes to produce and of the means by which he can produce it. In general, his technical effects are brilliantly carried off; and this is to say that the poem is generally successful. The abstractions are given substance and reality, occasionally by very minor touches, in several instances only by the music they produce, yet always enough to carry the movement of the poem forward; and the figures themselves are less static and statuesque than the figure, for example, of Mercy.

The concluding twenty-four lines of tetrameter couplets are an address to "*Music,* Sphere-descended Maid" asking why her "warm, Energic, Chaste, Sublime" inspiration was given Greece but denied to the present age:

> Where is thy native simple Heart,
> Devote to Virtue, Fancy, Art?
> . . . .
> O bid our Vain Endeavors cease,
> Revive the just Designs of *Greece,*
> Return in all thy simple State!
> Confirm the Tales Her Sons relate!   (104-118)

The point is not a plea for the Passions per se to inspire the poet, but rather for the passions in the "just Designs" of music, the most abstract and artificial of the arts—the art, therefore, most requiring the discipline of form, or, as Collins would have put it, of "Simplicity."

"The Passions" was, during the late eighteenth-century, the most popular of Collins' poems, and received almost universal praise. Langhorne insisted that ". . . upon the whole, there may be very little hazard in asserting that this is the finest ode in the English language," [34] and Dr. Johnson's objections to Collins' poems aroused a sharp rebuttal based on "The Passions": ". . . let Dr. Johnson, with all his erudition, produce me another Lyric ode equal to Collins on the Passions: indeed the frequent public recitals of this last-mentioned poem are a mark of its universally-acknowledged excellence. Lyric pieces are the more valuable, as few puny bards, in these degenerate days, are hardy enough to attempt anything in that bold style." [35]

Dickens provides evidence in *Great Expectations* that the practice of public recitations of the poem continued into the nineteenth century: "There was a fiction that Mr. Wopsle 'examined' the scholars, once a quarter. What he did on those occasions, was to turn up his cuffs, stick up his hair, and give us Mark Antony's oration over the body of Cæsar. This was always followed by Collins's Ode on the Passions, wherein I particularly venerated Mr. Wopsle as Revenge, throwing his blood-stain'd sword in thunder down, and taking the War denouncing trumpet with a withering look." [36]

The success of the poem is no doubt owing in part to the fact that the subject was in several ways of profound concern to Collins. Gilbert White tells us that Collins was passionately fond of music, and we have Collins' own word, in the letter to Hayes which I have already quoted,[37] that he was working on another ode on the subject. Of this ode it was thought until recently that no lines remained, but with the publication of Collins' *Drafts and Fragments* we may have, indeed, a fragment of the poem:

> When Glorious Ptolomy by Merit rais'd
> Successive sate on Ægypt's radiant Throne
> Bright Ptolomy, on whom, while Athens gaz'd
> She almost wish'd the Monarch once Her own
> Then Virtue own'd one Royal Heart;
> For loathing war, humanely wise
> For All the Sacred Sons of Art
> He bad the Dome of Science rise.
> The Muses knew the festal day
> And call'd by Pow'r Obsequiant came
> With all their Lyres and Chaplets gay
> They gave the *Fabric its immortal Name
> High oer the rest in Golden Pride
> The Monarch sate, and at his side
> His Fav'rite Bards—His Græcian Quire
> Who while the Roofs responsive Rung
> To many a Fife and many a tinkling Lyre
> Amid the Shouting Tribes in sweet succession Sung.
>
> (*Drafts and Fragments,* pp. 17-18)

I have performed as many tests as I could devise upon this fragment, but I have hit upon nothing which helps me decide whether

---

* The Μουσεῖον

it may have been written before or after the odes in the 1746 volume. The fact that it begins as a pretty clear imitation of Dryden's "Alexander's Feast" makes me think that Collins started it early in his writing career and then abandoned it; but on the other hand there is no compelling reason that I can see why it should not be late, and it might well, in a few more lines, have turned into an "Ode on the Music of the Grecian Theatre," straying farther away from Dryden in the process. I would guess that Collins had about this much of the poem on hand in November, 1750; that he had some vague design of turning the fragment into the projected ode he mentioned to Hayes; and that he needed the encouragement of Hayes or somebody else to overcome the lethargy imposed by already failing health. Whether or not he ever received such encouragement and completed another poem, now lost, we cannot know. On the whole the lines do not help us much in discussing Collins, except in so far as they may show Collins' interest in music—an interest which no doubt contributed materially to the success of "The Passions."

Does "The Passions" complete a single and coherent concept of poetic art, as Mr. Musgrove suggested in his very stimulating pair of articles? There he wished to show "that what the book, taken as a whole, is about, is the nature of the True Poet, as Collins conceived it, and that each Ode is descriptive of one of the qualities or circumstances essential to the attainment of the Poet's true stature.[38] That the volume is largely about some such thing I have already admitted. Certainly "Pity," "Fear," "Simplicity," and "On the Poetical Character" are concerned with art and the problems Collins had to face as a poet; certainly "The Manners" and "The Passions" belong in the same context. I wish I were convinced by Mr. Musgrove that the other poems belonged there too, but, ingenious as his theory is, I think he had to work too hard at it and I am not entirely convinced that "Collins's Poet must be 'modelled on the antique'; his 'soul' must be 'sincere' and devoted; he must be able to portray the 'manners' and emotions of men; he must shun the outworn way of traditions; his genius must be primarily lyrical in a way that recalls the lyrical poetry of Greece; and all these qualities must be crowned by the master-power of Imagination. He must be an active member of a society of free and brave men, and that society, for preference, should be at peace with its neighbours and in harmony with itself. Finally, he must go to Nature, particularly in her evening hours, for inspiration and solace." [39] Thus Mr. Musgrove.

If Collins had been asked to put his ideas on the nature of the True Poet in coherent form, they might well have run much as Mr. Musgrove has suggested. But I do not think we are justified in squeezing Collins' little book into the mold of what *we think* its author *might* have said. All we have is the book itself, and what it says as a whole—in so far as it is a whole—is at best very tenuous and vague. What it says about the True Poet is somewhat clearer, and seems to me to run something like this: "The True Poet in the act of creating partakes of the divine act of creation, which nowadays it is rarely if ever possible to emulate; his productions so inspired partake also of the world of divine forms of which the Greeks, in their drama and music, and Shakespeare and Milton have had true apprehension, and of which Simplicity is the prime attribute." I am not at all certain that the patriotic or political poems fit clearly into the context of the poems on art, though it is no doubt possible to deduce from them an idea of the sort of society Collins would have preferred, and hence of the society he would have found most congenial for poetic work. "Ode to Evening" may perhaps be taken as an example of the results of the poetic theory, although to say that Collins intended it to be so considered would be pure guess work.

The *Odes on Several Descriptive and Allegorical Subjects* is the work of a poet—not of a pre-Romantic poet nor of a neoclassical poet, but of a poet. With the *Poems by Mr. Gray,* 1768, Collins' *Odes* is beyond doubt the most important volume of poems published between the death of Pope and the advent of Blake, Burns, and the *Lyrical Ballads* at the end of the century.

VII *The Last Poems*

There remain only two of Collins' poems still to be discussed, of which only one, the "Ode Occasion'd by the Death of Mr. Thomson," 1748, was published during Collins' lifetime. There is no reason to doubt that this poem was the product of genuine grief at the death of a friend, but it is not an effusion of uncontrolled grief. To complain, as some have done, that the poem is cold is to misunderstand not only the poem but also the tradition of the

literary elegy. Collins' poem, for example, is clearly more a statement of personal grief than *Lycidas*, but this hardly makes it as
good a poem. The purpose of the ode is not to express grief but to
erect a memorial to Thomson, and in this it succeeds.

The opening line, "In yonder Grave a DRUID lies," has been
the subject of several unfavorable comments. From the time of
Mrs. Barbauld in the 1790's to that of Professor Garrod in 1928, it
was generally thought that the reference to Druids was inappropriate; recently the line has been defended.[40] It seemed to me a
good line the first time I read it; it seems so to me now; and I must
say I agree with those who think it fitting that Thomson, the Celtic nature poet and poet of *Liberty*, should be referred to in this
way connecting him with the long tradition of British liberty as
well as with the native growth of British poetry. As such, it is an
important part of the tribute Collins pays to his friend. It seems to
me an admirable elegy, certainly one of the best written in the
eighteenth century.

Briefly, what goes on in the poem is that the poet is boating on
the Thames, approaching Richmond, where Thomson is buried.

> IN yonder Grave a Druid lies
>   Where slowly winds the stealing Wave!
> The *Year's* best Sweets shall duteous rise
>   To deck *it's* POET's sylvan Grave!   (1-4)

Even in death the influence of the Druid poet is so strong as to
command Nature, who duteously decks his grave. The theme is
continued in the next stanza, where the attention shifts to those
who mourn him:

> In yon deep Bed of whisp'ring Reeds
>   His airy Harp shall now be laid,
> That He, whose Heart in Sorrow bleeds
>   May love thro' Life the soothing Shade.   (5-8)

The "airy Harp" is a reference, which Collins notes, to Canto I,
stanzas 40-41 of *The Castle of Indolence*. Thomson by his poetry
has taught his readers to "love thro' Life" the nature which he
celebrated. The reverberations of the word "Druid" are picked up

in the next stanza by "Woodland Pilgrim," and in stanza IV the
theme is generalized. "REMEMBRANCE oft shall haunt the
Shore"—and REMEMBRANCE, of course, is "all those who remember," who will "oft suspend the dashing Oar," as the boating
party now presumably does, "To bid his gentle Spirit rest." EASE
and HEALTH in the next stanza are, again, those persons who
possess such blessings; and these, as oft they retire "To breezy
Lawn, or Forest deep," will weep to remember the poet.

The central stanza of the eleven-stanza elegy is the traditional
elegiac turn, marked in *Lycidas* by "Alas! What books it with un-
cessant care," and in *Adonais* by "*He* will awake no more, oh,
never more!":

> But Thou, who own'st that Earthy Bed,
> Ah! what will ev'ry Dirge avail?
> Or Tears, which LOVE and PITY shed
> That mourn beneath the gliding Sail! (21-24)

We are reminded here again, we notice, of the dramatic situation
of the poem. The boat is gliding past the spot where Thomson is
buried. During the rest of the elegy, we are moving away from
the grave; and, as we do so, night is falling, as we find in stanza
IX. In the eighth stanza Collins addresses the Thames,

> . . . whose sullen Tide
> No sedge-crown'd SISTERS now attend
> Now waft we from the green Hill's Side
> Whose cold Turn hides the buried Friend! (29-32)

While in the fourth stanza it was Remembrance, the man who
remembered, who came to the grave, in stanza X it is the hinds
and shepherd-girls—those who owe only a simple allegiance to
the nature which Thomson vivified. And, while in the first stanza
it was Nature herself which paid tribute, in the last it is "the mus-
ing BRITON":

> Long, long, thy Stone and pointed Clay
> Shall melt the musing BRITON's Eyes,
> O! VALES, and WILD WOODS, shall HE say
> In yonder Grave YOUR DRUID lies! (41-44)

[*137*]

"Pointed" means "having the quality of penetrating or piercing the sensations, feeling, or mind" (*O.E.D.*). In the final stanza we are looking back toward the grave through the twilight, and Thomson is identified with the whole scene: "YOUR DRUID"—the poet-priest of Nature and of British liberty.

The elegy is simple, touching, sincere. It succeeds in what it sets out to do—to record with restraint an individual expression of grief and at the same time to leave a memorial to a true British poet. But its smooth lines conceal the double, or triple movement within the poem, the movement of thought reflected in the movement of the boat on the river, and by the approaching night. Professor Tillyard is the first commentator, I believe, to recognize the "Ode Occasion'd by the Death of Mr. Thomson" for the very fine poem it is; but even he, it seems to me, does not do full justice to the subtlety and art of the writing. The poem is deliberately underwritten to express a calmness of profound grief rather than the wild moanings of the nineteenth-century poetic convention. Never, except in "How Sleep the Brave" and in "Ode to Evening," did Collins display a greater control over his language or adapt it more perfectly to the matter at hand. The poem does not strike me as quite so nearly approaching greatness as the two best poems in the volume of *Odes*, yet I cannot find a line I object to or a word I would think better changed; and, as I study the poem, it seems to improve.

The "Ode on the Popular Superstitions of the Highlands of Scotland, Considered as the Subject of Poetry" might as properly be termed an "Epistle to Home." It was written apparently in 1749 as a parting gift to John Home, later to gain fame as author of *Douglas,* who had visited Collins, probably in Chichester, during the year. The details of its composition are hazy, but its subsequent history is interesting. Johnson mentions in his "Life of Collins" that upon the occasion of a visit by the Wartons to see Collins in Chichester, probably in 1754, "He shewed them . . . an ode inscribed to Mr. John Hume, on the superstitions of the Highlands; which they thought superiour to his other works, but which no search has yet found." [41] Some time early in the 1780's Dr. Alexander Carlyle, upon reading this statement, happened to remember that he had in his possession a manuscript in Collins' handwriting which fell into his hands in 1754 upon the death of a friend of his and Home's. "Soon after I found the poem," he wrote, "I shewed it to Mr. Home, who told me that it had been addressed to him by Mr. Collins, on his leaving London in the year 1749: that it was hastily composed and incorrect; but that he would one day find leisure to look it over with care." [42] Carlyle read the ode to the Royal Society of Edinburgh in 1784; and, when the society was preparing its first volume of *Transactions* for publication, it was thought appropriate to include this poem. It was accordingly published there in 1788 with lacunae filled with words or phrases by Carlyle, and with twenty-five lines of the missing fifth and part of the sixth stanzas supplied by Henry Mackenzie (author of *The Man of Feeling*). All deviations from Collins' manuscript were scrupulously marked with inverted commas, and Collins' own corrections on the manuscript were carefully recorded. Carlyle's additions, for want of anything better, are still admitted in brackets into the Oxford text of Collins.

Late in 1788 another edition of the poem appeared in London, edited by "a gentleman who, for the present, chooses not to publish his name," and purporting to be Collins' fair copy of the perfected poem which the gentleman had found in an old bureau drawer. There was a second edition the next year, but the gentleman never revealed his name. Professor W. C. Bronson has effectively demolished any claim this text had for consideration,[43] and we may safely ignore it—except as a curious example of mysteriously motivated literary fraud—even though it was the text used uncritically in most nineteenth-century editions. Ignoring the supposedly perfected text of the anonymous edition, however, means that we must consider the poem that we have as no more than the second draft of a work which Collins intended to revise further. The Edinburgh edition indicates nine verbal changes which Collins himself made in the manuscript in addition to two extensively rewritten passages, and it was necessary for Dr. Carlyle to supply seven words or phrases to fill lacunae where the fitting language had not yet occurred to the poet. We can assume that the missing stanza five and the first lines of stanza six were completed by Collins in some form or another on a leaf of the manuscript which Dr. Carlyle could not recover, although Carlyle could not remember whether his manuscript had ever included them. However that may be, we do not possess these lines, and it is as useless to speculate upon them as it is to speculate upon the text which the Wartons saw in 1754. What we have is a working draft of an uncompleted poem which it is neither logical nor fair to judge as though it were a final achievement.

The temptation is strong to judge the poem in just this way, for it seems to show an almost spectacular leap forward on Collins' part. Lowell said that the ode "contained the whole romantic school in the germ," [44] and it is from this standpoint that the poem has most often been discussed. To question the truth or falsity of such a point of view would lead us too far afield; we would have to know what Lowell's statement means; and, the more I think about it, the less I seem to know what it does mean. Yet it would be easy to acquiesce without thinking, for certainly Collins' verse does seem to anticipate Keats' and certainly the interests Collins displays are interests more fully developed poetically fifty years after his death than they were during his lifetime. What keeps me from following the easy, "pre-Romantic" line is the strong sense I have of the continuity within Collins' work. We know that Johnson, never having seen this poem, disapproved of the interest in "faeries, genii, giants and monsters" of which the "Ode on the Popular Superstitions" is a fruition. Interest in the Greek and Roman legends was perfectly respectable, and Collins in his earlier poetry showed a familiarity, though no unusual familiarity, with these. What was unusual was the transferring of this interest to the English Teutonic or Celtic legends, a step to which Collins' interest in early history might naturally have led him and one which the elder Warton had already taken before Collins wrote.

Even in rationalizing thus, however, we are ignoring the occasion for the poem. It is, as I said, really an "Epistle to Home," a letter addressed to a young Scot with literary ambitions with whom Collins had had enlivening conversations, and whose mind he had picked for information about his homeland. The first stanza is personal and informal, with its request that Home should remember a mutual friend who is about to be married and, indeed, Collins himself, who exhorts him to continue writing poetry. And what more natural than that the subjects of his poetry should come from the Scottish land itself? " 'Tis Fancy's land to which thou sett'st thy feet." The popular superstitions exist; they are therefore subjects for poetry. We are apt to overlook the way in which Collins recommends treating the subjects:

> Let thy sweet muse the rural faith sustain:
>   These are the themes of simple, sure effect,
> That add new conquests to her boundless reign,
> And fill, with double force, her heart-commanding strain.
> (32-35)

What he means by sustaining the "rural faith" is perhaps illuminated by the tenth stanza, where he speaks of the natives of St. Kilda. It is one of the best stanzas in the poem, and perhaps, because of the poetic quality, the prose content is not always observed:

> . . . Go, just, as they, their blameless manners trace!
> Then to my ear transmit some gentle song
>   Of those whose lives are yet sincere and plain
>
> .   .   .   .
>
> Thus blest in primal innocence they live,
>   Suffic'd and happy with that frugal fare
> Which tasteful toil and hourly danger give.
>   Hard is their shallow soil, and bleak and bare;
> Nor ever vernal bee was heard to murmur there!   (158-171)

This is the rural faith; it is primitivism, an old acquaintance to anyone who has read much in the scholarship published during the past thirty years devoted to eighteenth-century subjects. It is so closely connnected with eighteenth-century thought that some of us by a Pavlovian reaction start babbling "primitivism" as soon as the eighteenth century is mentioned. It may be "pre-Romantic"; but, if it is, then in that sense so are Shakespeare and the Parthenon. And in the twelfth stanza we get another eighteenth-century cliché:

> IN scenes like these, which, daring to depart
>   From sober truth, are still to nature true,
> And call forth fresh delight to fancy's view,
>   Th'heroic muse employ'd her TASSO's art!   (188-191)

[141]

Collins may here extend the idea of truth to nature as a criterion
for poetry, yet he might have reminded himself, too, that to copy
Homer is to copy nature, and Homer is not without marvels and
prodigies; nor, as Collins himself points out, is that emulable
Ancient, Shakespeare. He had already, in the eleventh stanza,
hedged on the matter of these subjects:

> NOR need'st thou blush, that such false themes engage
>> Thy gentle mind, of fairer stores possest;
> For not alone they touch the village breast,
>> But fill'd in elder time th'historic page.
> There SHAKESPEARE's self, with ev'ry garland crown'd,
>> In musing hour, his wayward sisters found,
> And with their terrors drest the magic scene.   (172-178)

The themes are false, but their use is justified even by a mind "of
fairer stores possest" on the clear neoclassical ground of ancient
authority—a critical approach, if I may call it that, to these
themes which was hardly revolutionary.

I confess that I may appear to be trying too hard to force this
poem into a neat, eighteenth-century context; but, if that is so, it
is because I do not see any need to stretch it into a nineteenth-
century one. That, if one must seek resemblances, it resembles in
its verse texture and subject some poems of the early 1800's more
than it resembles *MacFlecknoe,* it would be impossible to deny,
even if there were any reason to do so; that it therefore belongs
somehow to any age other than its own it is ridiculous to assert,
though some have made the asseveration. If the "Ode to Liberty"
is an eighteenth-century poem, then so is the "Ode on the Popular
Superstitions of the Highlands of Scotland, Considered as the
Subject of Poetry," and it is so no less in its verse form than its
subject.

It is the development perceptible in Collins' verse which is most
notable. Here we are apt to be misled by trying to fit the ode into
the Pindarick convention, where it does not belong. The form is
stanzaic and reminds us of the long strophe and antistrophe of
"Ode to Liberty," yet the intention of the poem is not vocative in
the same way. Collins is not addressing the popular superstitions,
though in the last stanza he does hail the "scenes that o'er my soul

prevail"; he is until this stanza addressing Home, and addressing him in a personal, intimate tone, not in the "sublime" manner used in addressing a personification. The occasion of the poem called for a sort of verse Collins had used before only in "Hanmer," where, as it is hardly necessary to point out, the occasion was so different as hardly to be comparable. Even these facts, however, do not account for the new, unaffected straightforwardness and smoothness of the verse. There is none of the complicated syntax, the suspended periods, the indefinite reference of pronouns, which are characteristic of most of the earlier poems. The grammar and the sense proceed amicably hand in hand. There is also an increase in the number of run-on lines; Collins is thinking in terms of a larger unit than he had heretofore mastered.

On the other hand, some of the mannerisms of diction obtrude themselves more noticeably. There is an increase in the noun-"y" adjective: "Wintry," "dreary," "wat'ry," "quaggy," "lusty," "rosy," "moody." All of these appear in the fourth stanza, though that is the greatest concentration. He also developed a fondness for negative forms such as "unmindful" and "untainted," the ode containing no less than eleven unusual examples of such words. It is possible that some of these verbal "tics" might have been eliminated in a thorough revision, but I cannot believe very strongly in the possibility. The question is not important, for the point is that, out of the commonplaces of the style familiar to him, Collins was evolving a refined and highly personal medium—as does every good poet. He did not work long enough—as Keats only barely did—to hammer his style into perfection, but in the "Ode on the Popular Superstitions of the Highlands" we get a tantalizing glimpse of what that perfection might have been.

We can get another glimpse of Collins' poetic intellect at work by examining the way in which he used his sources. The Edinburgh edition of 1788 pointed out his use of Martin Martin's *A Description of the Western Isles of Scotland, Circa 1695,* of which a 1716 reprint of the 1703 edition was current during Collins' lifetime. The volume is still fascinating reading, and it is easy to understand why Collins, who was no doubt first directed to it by Home's conversation, found snatches of it coming into his mind as he wrote his epistle to Home. Martin was not a poet, and he approached the question of second sight, for example, with a simple skepticism that was later converted to belief. Collins reduces a thirty-five page passage in Martin[45] to a few lines in stanza four:

> Or if in sports, or on the festive green,
> Their [piercing] glance some fated youth descry,
> Who, now perhaps in lusty vigour seen
> And rosy health, shall soon lamented die.
> For them the viewless forms of air obey,
> Their bidding heed, and at their beck repair.
> They know what spirit brews the stormful day,
> And heartless, oft like moody madness stare
> To see the phantom train their secret work prepare.   (61-69)

There is nothing in Martin about "For them the viewless forms of air obey," and the last five lines are purely Collins' invention—that is, so far as Martin is concerned; we cannot, of course, recapture Home's conversation. Similarly, in a short, dry passage Martin recounts that sixty Scots, Irish, and Norwegian kings lie buried on Icolmkill.[46] In his ninth stanza Collins works his particular magic upon this information:

> Or thither where beneath the show'ry west
> The mighty kings of three fair realms are laid:
> Once foes, perhaps, together now they rest.
> No slaves revere them, and no wars invade:
> Yet frequent now, at midnight's solemn hour,
> The rifted mounds their yawning cells unfold,
> And forth the monarchs stalk with sov'reign pow'r
> In pageant robes, and wreath'd with sheeny gold,
> And on their twilight tombs aerial council hold.   (146-154)

That this is "Romantic" there can be no doubt. That it is for that reason remarkable in an age which devoured Blair's *Grave* and Walpole's *The Castle of Otranto* is more doubtful.

What we have in this poem, as in the best of Collins' other poems, is an extraordinarily perceptive, individual response to poetic and intellectual vibrations in the air at the time. Collins was not here, nor in any of his other work, a bold innovator, but he was a sensitive recording instrument whose sensitivity and art made it possible for him to appear to be foreshadowing the future of English poetry.

[144]

CHAPTER 4

Collins as Poet

THE poet who wrote "Ode to Evening" and "How Sleep the Brave" would be interesting if he had written nothing else. So few poets have produced two such poems that one who did will never be wholly neglected. But Collins is the author of an *œuvre*, however slight, and about that whole body of work it is not easy to make a satisfactory general statement. When we come to what must be the final duty of any critic—to answer the question, "How good is this poetry?"—we find the temptation very great merely to take refuge in a formula: "Two poems are great; two or three additional poems are very good; the others are either indifferently competent or, in a few cases, bad." Such an answer permits us to return the book to the shelf with the feeling that we have said something, but it does not sufficiently illuminate the poems or help us to know what to think about their author as a poet. The question, however, must be faced; and in this chapter I shall approach it somewhat circuitously through discussions of those experiences Collins valued, and of some of the sources of his poetry, to which I will add a few words on his fame and his possible influence on several poetical successors. For no matter what approach we may make to such monolithic poets as Shakespeare and Milton, a poet such as Collins is best seen in the perspective of a literary landscape.

I *Collins as Man of Feeling*

Collins was a poet, not a philosopher, moralist, story-teller, sage, or prophet; and it is as a poet that he must be judged—as a man who is able to make public in words a vision ultimately private, and to make us believe the vision. Pope did this, and so did Keats; Chaucer did it, and so did Dylan Thomas. The first requisite for the poet is that he have mastered his language, his technique; the second, that he see and feel intensely and clearly. To say this is not necessarily to say that the poet must be clear about what he sees: a clear vision of chaos is as much a clear vision as is a revelation of the planetary motion. But I cannot think of any first-rate poem which seems to me vague about what it is getting at, and which does not reveal its author's own vision. This is as true of the "Prologue" to the *Canterbury Tales* as it is of "Ode to a Grecian Urn"; of the "Epistle to Arbuthnot" as of "The Force that through the Green Fuse Drives the Flower."

The question in the case of Collins is not primarily one of the poet's technique. In the analyses of "Ode to Evening" and of "The Passions" particularly, we have seen that Collins' ability to manipulate his language was equal to any demands he put upon it, and in the "Ode on the Popular Superstitions of the Highlands" we have observed how this technique was developing and turning into a more flexible and sensitive instrument. If the technique in the earlier poems seems limited, it is because Collins put limited demands upon it.

Had Collins' technique been different—that is, free from certain restrictions of eighteenth-century poetic theory—the demands might have been greater, but that is hardly a question into which we can enter here, posing as it does the "chicken-or-the-egg" problem as to the relation of what a poet wants to say to the way he says it. The verbal patterns a poet's ear has heard and is accustomed to hear inevitably have a large bearing upon what his imagination is able to fit into those patterns. The verbal patterns Collins heard were, as is the case with every poet, those of his own time; and he did not live long enough to make any very important alterations except those minor ones inherently possible within those patterns. Some of these minor changes were important, however, not only for themselves and for the possible (though certainly not provable) influence they may have had on a few later poets, but also as indicating the greater demands Collins was putting on his technique.

For the things a poet wants to say—and he a man of strong feelings—can be conceived of, I suspect, as being like a flood within a channeled river. The natural tendency of the river is to run within its channel, which may be compared to the inherited technique of the poet; but, under the force of flood waters, the river may have to cut a new channel; and, forced by a flood of perceptions or feelings which his channel of technique will not contain, the poet must either dam them up or create a new technical channel into which they can flow. Collins' perceptions and feelings were never at flood so far as we can tell from the flow of his poetry, yet this does not necessarily mean there was not a great tide of feeling. A channel may be contained and still run deep; the technique inherited may be adequate for an immense flow of passion.

If this analogy, which I may have carried farther than can be useful, is not so clear as it might be, it is possibly because I am trying to explain something about Collins—and Collins himself was not always entirely clear as to certain of his own feelings. The several occasions on which Collins exclaims "Teach me but once like him to feel" or "If but from Thee I hope to feel" make us wonder, indeed, whether Collins thought himself deficient in emotion. Very clearly he actively sought emotional experience, but also, somewhat less clearly, he found such experience only in imagination. Johnson complains soundly that "perhaps, while he was intent upon description he did not sufficiently cultivate sentiment." We can surely be grateful that Collins did not, like a truly minor poet, cultivate false sentiment; what he does feel, he feels honestly and intensely. But we cannot but be aware that the range of this feeling was limited. I mentioned earlier the unusual circumstance that Collins no where treats love more than casually, except within the artifice of the *Oriental Eclogues*. This fact can probably be taken as evidence of his honesty, for at least he did not, like Shenstone, for example, maunder on about purely contrived emotions. In fact, there is nowhere in his work evidence for emotion of any sort directed toward human beings, except for feelings of the grief, carefully contained within his technique, that he displays in the elegy on Thomson.

I do not know how to explain this fact about Collins' poetry. We do not know enough about Collins' life, or about the relation of any man's creative capacity to the culture in which it must operate, to see what was wrong in Collins' case—if we can truly say anything was wrong. All assumptions about what other people do or "ought to" feel spring from the assumption that everyone does or "ought to" feel much as we do, an assumption which I would not easily grant. That Collins did not feel just as most men feel is obvious. That he wanted to feel more as other men did is very likely, to my mind, the meaning of "Teach me but once like him to feel." That it would have been better for him or for poetry had he felt differently is a proposition we can have no reason to make. We can only wish he had lived long enough in good health that he himself might have come to recognize the value of his own mode of feeling. It was on this point alone that he was not clear.

We cannot doubt that his particular feelings were intense. He could feel strongly, for example, about things patriotic; and he could feel with peculiar intensity about art. But it is to be noticed that we find these emotions, quite in accordance with his inherited technical apparatus, couched in terms of generalities instead of finding the generalities embodied in highly human and personal terms, as was so often the case in Pope's poetry. In fact we seem to have in Collins the unique (so far as I know) example of a logical consequence of neoclassic esthetic philosophy: an example of a man who seems to have been genuinely stirred only by esthetic emotions, by generalities.

Mr. Murry says that "the danger of this intense concentration upon a purely literary purpose is an impoverishment of the sensibility," [1] but this is so only if we insist upon a certain conventional kind of sensibility. Collins, as I have said, may have felt his own sensibility limited; yet, in the spheres in which it operated, it was extraordinarily intense, and produced poetry upon themes not usually subjected to such intensity. His feelings may have been impoverished in areas in which human sensibility most commonly operates, but it was tremendously enriched and articulate in certain possible spheres of perception which most of us are never able to enter. This ability accounts for the remoteness, the odd savor of such poems as "Ode on the Poetical Character" and "Ode to Liberty," and it is the application to nature of this strangely (to us) directed sensibility which accounts for the uniqueness of "Ode to Evening." To say that the sensibility which produced these poems was "impoverished" is perhaps only to say that it is not like our own; it is to take Collins literally by his own words. That he may have wanted to feel differently is not surprising; the man who is different from his fellows usually regrets the fact, even though he may ostensibly glory in the difference. But

for us to wish that Collins had had the feelings of any man is
strangely to undervalue what we have. The very limitation of the
range of his feeling is his peculiar strength.

Collins cannot be concerned primarily with nature, then, in the
sense taken either by Pope or Wordsworth but rather, as Mr.
Woodhouse says,[2] with a world of ideal forms made real by the
divine act of imagination. These are rarified realms difficult for
us to enter, as every commentator on Collins has realized. If I
had any particular reason to think Collins had studied Plato, I
should be tempted to try to explicate his world in Platonic terms.
What Platonism he had I should guess he got from Spenser and
Shaftesbury; but I am afraid it does not seem to me a subject
worth following out except for purposes of curiosity. The idea of
Platonic "reality" is not hard to get; and, once he got it, Collins
put it to his own uses without pursuing it formally or in depth.
Or rather, since it was so clearly an idea highly congenial to him,
he pursued it in his own way, as we have seen in our examina-
tions of the odes on "The Poetical Character" and "Liberty." Certainly this sort of rather superficial Platonism gives us an insight
into the way Collins saw his world, and it is a major fact about his
poetry; but, having pointed it out, I am not sure we can honestly
do much more with it.

It was the interest in ideal forms, however, which may explain
—if it needs explaining—Collins' interest in painting and sculpture; certainly the particular bent of his concern with the other
arts may be guessed more clearly by reference to "The Passions."
I have already mentioned how, as early as the *Epistle to Hanmer,*
Collins seemed to be striving after sculpturesque effects. That he
tended to think in terms of such effects is further indicated by reference to that letter to John Gilbert Cooper written in 1747 which
I have already mentioned. Collins is discussing their proposed
journal:

. . . You found by my last that I propos'd the more literary papers
should fall under the name of Polèmon, and the more lusory or Comic
under that of Philethus. In order to Hint this at the head of the Paper
I shall have a Medallion engrav'd of two Elegant Heads a l'antique
thus [*drawing of two heads in profile facing right*] (Don't you think
'em a l'antique?) over the lower part of the necks of which there shall

be a veil thrown, from under which a little *Art* shall appear writing on a Roman scroll, and a *Satyr* either in contrast holding up another, or writing on part of the same [I] suppose the veil be upheld by *Friendship,* who may at the same time point to the Relievo of the Medallion while she discovers the ornaments of the base by supporting the veil. . . .³

Collins' drawing is crudely suggestive of a Roman coin, but it sufficiently shows what he had in mind; and the description of Art, Friendship, and so on shows us that he was actually visualizing a meaning in these graphic terms, not just inventing a design. This sort of design was a common feature of eighteenth-century books, an indication again of how much of a piece with his age Collins really was and of how much he was influenced by what he casually encountered around him; for, if the arrangement of the personified abstractions in his odes occasionally seems to be designed for a statuary group or a frieze, as in the case of the figure of Mercy, it seems as often to be visualized in terms of an allegorical painting which can remind us of these fantastic decorations on title pages and head- or tailpieces of eighteenth-century books. The design on page 99 of the Oxford edition of the poems of Gray and Collins is a convenient example. The ode on "The Passions" constantly suggests such scenes. We have seen, in the passages from *Drafts and Fragments* quoted in our discussion of "Ode to Evening" how Collins actually looked at natural scenery through the eyes of art. Art was more real to him than life simply because it approached more nearly to the "Platonic" reality, though Collins nowhere says this. At the time he was writing, the doctrine *ut pictura poesis* was being reaffirmed by Joseph Spence and others, but no one more thoroughly made it an animating force of poetic creation than Collins.

Professor Wylie Sypher, in a most stimulating article,⁴ has suggested that Collins' obviously visual arrangement (or disarrangement) of the figures in his odes can best be related to the rococo art of contemporary France, and may more appropriately be called *genre pittoresque* than "Romantic." Collins' poetry is, says Mr. Sypher, a representative of the rococo, just as is the work of his contemporary, Chippendale, who, indeed, could well have taken designs for clock-cases, pier glasses, or girandoles from Col-

lins' poems. This is to say again that Collins' poetry is very much
of its time. I do not agree that Collins is quite so disorderly, quite
so surrealistic (Mr. Sypher's own word, and in some respects an
apt one) as Mr. Sypher contends; but I am certainly willing to
accept his perception that Collins' poetry is an example of the
rococo in verse.

The rococo in verse, however, is not the same thing as the
rococo in decoration. Chippendale's designs veer toward a for-
malized unbalance, even toward that disorder which became
almost a precept of rococo art, though never one accepted by
rigorous estheticians; but it must be a somewhat academic conception of order which finds a disorder in Collins' poems. The
formal poetic theory of the time was, indeed, concerned with
"correctness," even though in poetry and in other arts a strong current of taste was running toward "wildness"—the characteristic of
the Pindarick. An obvious esthetic tension was set up. The problem was somehow to contain the wildness within a formal limit
without, at the same time, actually resolving the tension which
was the esthetic virtue of the Pindarick form on those relatively
few occasions when it was successful. This tension is more easily
felt in reading the odes than it is described, and it is hardly an effect achieved by accident. In fact, it would have been fatal to the
poetry, or rendered Collins incapable of writing at all, if he had
not been quite clear about the effect he was hoping to achieve.
The "Ode to Liberty," for example, as we have seen, has a perfectly explicable logical structure within which the "rococo" details move. The "wildness" is mostly a matter of syntax and of the
evocation of "wild" scenes, such as that describing the separation
of the British Isles from the Continent. The structure of the poem,
formally, is secure and regular; but within that structure there
are strong eddies of sense and feeling which seem to contradict
the strict formal façade. The only time when Collins abandons the
strictest of outward forms is in "The Passions," and there he devotes particular attention, as we have observed, to internal de-
vices of form—to rhyme and rhythmic sound links which tie the
poem together. In the "Ode on the Popular Superstitions" he uses
a long stanza which gives him a greater freedom than he had permitted himself in the earlier odes. The unfinished state of the
poem does not allow us to comment very accurately on the way

Collins handled that stanza, but certainly there is no reason to complain about the disorder of the poem, even though a few of the stanzas are not perfectly regular. There is, indeed, less "wildness" in this poem than in earlier ones.

But even more to the point is the unity of feeling within the poems. Only once, I think, in the "Ode to Peace" was Collins not sure what he really felt, but only parroting what he felt he ought to feel. It is his only dishonest poem. In all the others, if we stop to think, we can be conscious of a highly focused feeling. Collins may have wanted Shakespeare to teach him how to feel, but the fact is that, within his own realm of feeling, he was perfectly secure and did not need to be taught anything. The unity of feeling behind the poems controls the tension between the "wildness" and correctness, and this control of disparate forces, in turn, is the source of the unique quality of his poetry.

The "wildness" itself must be understood not merely in terms of the conventions of a literary form, even though it was the attitude prescribed to writers of the Pindarick. Why Collins valued it and no doubt sought actively to feel it can be discovered only if we understand the implications of the conclusion to "Ode on the Poetical Character":

> My trembling Feet his guiding Steps pursue;
>   In vain—Such Bliss to One alone,
>   Of all the Sons of Soul was known,
>   And Heav'n, and *Fancy*, kindred Pow'rs,
>   Have now o'erturn'd th'inspiring Bow'rs,
> Or curtain'd close such Scene from ev'ry future View.   (71-76)

The reference in the first quoted line is to Milton, the archetype of the poetical character, who alone among moderns had possessed the "Cest of amplest Pow'r" of the creative imagination, which is the primary fact of art. The poet despairs of attaining this god-like heritage—literally god-like, we remember, for in terms of the poem it is the primary creative power associated with God's creation of the universe. It does, therefore, transcend the limits of the immediate and actual and creates its own worlds of intense experience, of "wildness." [5] These experiences, however, are purely of the creative spirit and are concerned, at least as far as we can deduce from Collins' poetry, primarily with the ideal forms of life, not with life itself. They are the experiences of art. This fact may, at least in part, account for the lack of conventional passion in Collins' poems. The experiences he valued, and those most valuable as poetic material, were not the experiences which could be referred to so mundane an event as love.

II   *Collins' Sources*

Before I return to the question of a critical judgment of Collins' poetry, there are a few other subjects to be discussed: his sources and the works that influenced him. I have already mentioned many of Collins' sources in discussing particular poems. The most evident sources are Milton and the earlier English poets. Shakespeare must be counted a major influence, and also Spenser. Exactly how deeply he read in earlier English literature we cannot possibly say. Thomas Warton mentions that Collins had made an extensive collection of early books, and that Collins had suggested to him several obscure sources for Shakespeare, but of the very minor English poets only Fairfax can be cited with any assurance as a possible source, for certainly Collins had read his translation of Tasso's *Gerusalemme Liberata*.

He was also, naturally, influenced by later English poets—by Dryden for the form of the Pindarick, by Pope in the *Oriental Eclogues* and *Epistle to Hanmer*, and by Thomson most obviously in "Ode to Liberty" but also no doubt in those hundreds of subtle ways which only friendship makes possible. I have emphasized throughout my discussion the influence of the Wartons, and who would dare try to count the possible influence of such poets no doubt read by Collins as Prior or Young, whose *Night Thoughts* appeared in plenty of time to have been reflected in Collins' *Odes*. Not that anything in Collins reminds me of the *Night Thoughts*, but it is the sort of "new poetry" which we can hardly imagine Collins to have missed reading. And what a poet reads is almost bound in one way or another to influence him, if only by determining him never to write in this way or that.

On the whole question of sources and influences upon Collins it would be profitless to repeat the work Mr. Ainsworth has already so industriously performed.[6] We should take into account when considering the subject that Collins belonged to a group which shared literary interests, and we may suppose that the members of this group showed and read their poems to one another and communicated their enthusiasms. We must particularly remember also that this group did not yet have the modern conception of originality, a conception imposed upon literature since the nineteenth century, and, as it seems to me, one of the most crippling literary conventions ever conceived. Collins and his contemporaries were much freer to make use of a vital past as a part of their present than authors today, and Collins felt freer to adopt what struck him than would a twentieth-century poet. He did annotate a few of his conscious borrowings, but a detailed untangling of them from one another and from those of which he may not have been conscious does not really lead us very far toward understanding anything very important about his poetry.

I should like to comment further on one more of Collins' sources, however—his use of the Classics. Familiarity with the Latin authors was an accepted part of any early eighteenth-century poet's technical and spiritual equipment, and I have already mentioned the pervasive influence of Virgil in the period. I hardly need mention also the importance of Horace, particularly of his odes. J. A. K. Thomson mentions that the qualities of these, strictly inimitable in English, were always admired in ages such as the eighteenth century which understood them, and that in a poem such as "Ode to Evening" Collins succeeds in capturing something of the skill in ordering words, the quietness of statement controlling deep emotion, and the conciseness and economy which mark Horace's poetry. "Collins," he says, "is one of the most classical of our poets when he writes in this style, and [in "Ode to Evening"] and elsewhere, as in the ode on Thomson's death and the "Dirge in *Cymbeline*," he has been able to give his verse some of the *curiosa felicitas*—that natural-seeming grace which is the result of art—that was anciently attributed to Horace." [7] So high a compliment from so eminent a voice needs no embellishment.

Latin poetry was a standard acquirement of the age, but Greek was relatively rare until about the middle of the century, when there was a Greek revival and Gray, Akenside, and Thomas Warton, along with Collins, all became proficient in that tongue. It is certainly possible that the elegiac, retrospective tone of much of the verse of the late 1740's and early 1750's may in part be traced to that vein of underlying sadness and questing which pervades the Greek tragedies and much of the Greek Anthology, and which might well have had a special appeal in the mid-eighteenth century.[8]

More pertinent for us, however, is something even more vague. That Collins may have known and been influenced by Pindar in the original, as well as by the Greek Anthology, and by the dramatists, we can take for granted, although these influences, if laid before us in parallel passages, would not mean any more or less, except as a curiosity, than the influences of Milton and Shakespeare. Yet there is a pervasive quality that I may point out in Collins' works, and for which the influence of the Greeks may in part be accountable: the concept of "form" in art which Collins writes about in the "Ode to Simplicity." I think this love of what he calls Simplicity is allied to his love of Classical, especially Greek, literature and to what (probably little) he knew of Greek art. It can be explained only in terms of the sort of natural affinity which is ultimately as inexplicable as any other kind of love. Collins' inspiration seemed naturally to shape itself into Greek forms; and, amid the profuseness of his personifications and the sometimes strained attempts at "wildness," there seems alway perceptible the effort to preserve the simplicity—the form—of outline which is so profoundly, so radically Grecian. This is nothing which the citation of parallels can ever prove, and yet I feel it to be true. Collins' art seems to me to be Classical in a profound sense—Classical more than neoclassical, perhaps more Horatian than truly Greek, but owing a deep spiritual debt to Hellas, a debt which we may count adequately repaid by "How Sleep the Brave" and "Ode to Evening."

III   *Collins and Gray: The Growth of Fame*

The reader will have been able to gather from what I have already written the essential facts necessary for a history of Collins' fame during the eighteenth century. It is fairly accurately reflected in the sequence of editions of his works, beginning with the collection published in *The Poetical Calendar* for 1763 by Fawkes and Woty with the comment by Johnson. Dodsley in 1748 had inserted several of Collins' poems in the second edition of his *Collection,* but even so it cannot be said that Collins was very widely known in the 1760's even after Langhorne's edition in 1765. These printings, however, kept his poetry accessible and no doubt did much to make possible the wider appreciation which came later.

Before I turn to a brief discussion of Collins' later reputation and possible influence there is another matter which I must touch upon: the comparison between Collins and Gray. The two poets have been compared at least since 1782, when a correspondent in *The Gentleman's Magazine* pointed out, in connection with objections to Johnson's criticisms of Gray: "In the Elegy, so generally thought original, he has borrowed much from a contemporary poet: whosoever compares it with Collins' Ode to Evening will find such marks of particular imitation as are of more importance than all those with which Gray ornamented the bottom of his pages, exclusive of the general similarity of design of the two poems." The correspondent points out three instances of borrowing, and then goes on to remark: "Collins has had the misfortune not to please Dr. J. His works also are encumbered with a mass of absurd criticisms written by his editor Langhorne, only to piece out a volume, and his four eclogues are mere trash; yet a part of his Odes will, notwithstanding, command the admiration of mankind, as long as poetical genius or poetical taste shall remain in the world." [9]

The necessity of identifying Collins as "a contemporary poet" points up the fact that in 1782 Gray was much better known, which may still be the case, though the works of the two poets are embalmed together between the blue covers of the Oxford edition. By the early nineteenth century, however, opinion had actually begun to favor Collins. In 1802 Henry Crabb Robinson wrote to his brother Thomas: "Wordsworth's Ballads have infinite Metrical beauty, *Gray* too understood the Secret of Verse making—As a poet I look on him now as of very inferior Merit, he is not the Tithe of Collins whose poems I lately read as if I had never read them before—His Odes are wonderfully great & beautiful but I consider Wordsworth as our first living Poet. . . ." [10] And Sir John Taylor Coleridge, Coleridge's nephew, reported that his uncle "thought Collins had more genius than Gray, who was a singular instance of a man of taste, poetic feeling, and fancy, without imagination." [11] In 1880 Swinburne carried this view to the extreme of saying, "But it is not a question which admits of debate at all, among men qualified to speak on such matters, that as a lyric poet Gray was not worthy to unloose the latchets of [Collins'] shoes." [12]

I think it would hardly be necessary to compare Gray and Collins at all had not the issue been forced upon us by such remarks. The reason why it has been forced upon us is probably not very subtle. Gray and Collins were the two men who wrote great lyrics in a long age not notable for lyric poetry. In the last hundred and fifty years lyric poetry has exercised the greatest appeal to most readers and critics. Gray and Collins, then, have been spotlighted, so to speak, in what most of these readers and critics have considered the dimness of eighteenth-century poetic inspiration; and, because they were the only poets seen, they were naturally compared.

A comparison between them does not lead us very far. They were as different as Coleridge and Byron, and displayed something of the same sort of similarities. They both sought some kind of inspiration from the past, though Gray was much more the scholar and much more interested in the particular appurtenances of the British past than was Collins. This sort of similarity is superficial. The important thing to be said in a comparison, which tends to bear out Swinburne's view, though I could not state it so strongly, is that Gray succeeded—really succeeded—only once. His poems other than the "Elegy" would hardly be noticed if it were not for that poem, and I am afraid poems like "The Fatal Sisters" and "The Bard" are most interesting as symptoms of something happening to the body poetic. After the "Elegy" Gray simply became odd and then odder, and there is no reason to think anything could have changed him. After the *Odes on Several Descriptive and Allegoric Subjects* Collins wrote another poem which, as we have it, is almost the equal of anything in his earlier volume and which, if we had the perfect copy, we might well see to have been the best thing he ever did. Collins had a sustainable inspiration; I do not see that Gray had. It is not quite fair to say that the "Elegy" was a sublime fluke, yet I am tempted to say that it was—but without in any way intending a denigration of that great poem.

Between the "Elegy" and "Ode to Evening" I would hesitate to choose, again because they are such entirely different products of entirely different eighteenth-century inspirations. All they have in common is a tone of quietness, perhaps of melancholy (though I would have to qualify greatly that latter word, particularly as applied to "Ode to Evening"), the fact that both have to do with evening, and the fact that both were written in the mid-eighteenth century when nothing else of that kind was written so well. The differences between the poems are more important than the similarities, and the chief difference is that the "Elegy" is much more the conventional sort of mid-century poem, but embodies those conventions in marble instead of foam. It is above all else a moral poem, a didactic poem; and it shows better than anything else in English that to moralize in verse is not to grasp a dead hand. Gray's object is the Horatian one of instruction and delight. "Ode to Evening," on the other hand, is a poem of the senses; its appeal is to our senses and not to our sensibilities. It is a poem profoundly about art which does not *say* anything about art. In this single way it is much the more "modern" of the two poems. The difference between the poems is radical, and it is an enlightening difference for our understanding of Collins; the similarities between the poems are accidental and apt to be misleading.

Gray may himself have sensed the essential difference. Shortly after the publication of the books by Collins and Warton, he wrote in a letter to Warton dated December 27, 1746:

Have you seen the Works of two young Authors, a Mr Warton & a Mr Collins, both Writers of Odes? it is odd enough, but each is half of a considerable Man, & one the Counter-Part of the other. the first has but little Invention, very poetical choice of Expression, & a good Ear. the second, a fine Fancy, model'd upon the Antique, a bad Ear, great Variety of Words, & Images with no choice at all. they both deserve to last some Years, but will not.[13]

Coming from the author of "The Fatal Sisters," Gray's remarks on Collins sound strange; but "The Fatal Sisters" was fifteen years in the future. Coming from the man who at the time was working on the *Elegy Written in a Country Churchyard*, the remarks are slightly more comprehensible. In any case, they did not indicate a very happy reception for Collins' poems, and in this, we know, they forecast truly. It was not until Johnson's *Lives of the Poets* brought several defenses of Collins and until the discovery and printing of the "Ode on the Popular Superstitions of the Highlands" that his fame began to be established; and, by the beginning of the nineteenth century, it was secure. No one since that time has challenged Collins' right to his small place in anthologies and surveys of English poetry; and, since the 1790's, there has been, I believe, some edition of his poems continuously in print.[14]

IV   *Collins and the Romantic Poets*

The fact that Collins has been continuously in print for a century and three quarters means that he has during that time been continuously available as an influence on other poets. I do not see any reason to believe that he was a very important influence on any very important poet, but he was read, and perhaps one or two of his lines were remembered at a crucial moment. It seems to me that many of the parallels and supposed influences which Mr. Ainsworth has pointed out are rather strained; and, except that it may show that Collins was being read, I do not see that the fact that Chatterton, Charlotte Smith, and William Lisle Bowles echo Collins need concern us much.

What may concern us more is the possible effect a reading of Collins may have had on the great poets at the beginning of the nineteenth century. It is in relation to these poets that Collins has most frequently been studied, and this fact forces me to digress for a few words on the subject of the "pre-Romantics." Collins lived before the "Romantics"; therefore, he is "pre-Romantic." In this sense of the term Johnson and Pope must also be "pre-Romantic," while Crabbe, presumably, would have to be some kind of "Romantic." Such a purely chronological use of the word is clearly preposterous. But the other sense of "pre-Romantic" is invidious, implying as it does that Collins, Gray, and Thomson are interesting or worth studying only, or primarily, for the ways in which Wordsworth, Shelley, and Keats built upon or drew upon their poetic legacy. The epithet tends to discourage the study of the poets for themselves in a way which we are not discouraged from studying, for example, Vaughan, Herbert, or Lovelace, who are not pre- or post- anything but are allowed to be themselves, even though they may have influenced someone after them. I wish to study Collins' poetry for itself, and I contend that its interest as poetry is neither increased nor diminished by what other poets made or failed to make of it later. That the "Romantics" made or failed to make something of Collins' poetry is an interesting fact, but it has nothing to do with the study of that poetry.

With this perhaps somewhat bad-tempered preface, I am ready to concede that Wordsworth seems to have liked Collins, although I am not at all sure we can point to any assured "influence" of Collins' poetry on Wordsworth's. Wordsworth made some suggestions to Dyce when the latter was preparing his edition of Collins, and at least four times he mentions Collins' poetry, though without expressing any very avid enthusiasm. His most glowing tribute to Collins—a tribute which glows a bit coldly at best when we remember the enthusiastic vein which Wordsworth could command on greater occasions—is the little poem "Remembrance of Collins: composed upon the Thames near Richmond," in which he concludes:

> Now let us, as we float along,
> For *him* suspend the dashing oar;
> And pray that never child of song
> May know that Poet's sorrows more.
> How calm! how still! the only sound,
> The dripping of the oar suspended!
> —The evening darkness gathers round
> By virtue's holiest Powers attended.

It was, indeed, Collins' elegy on Thomson which seems to have impressed Wordsworth most deeply, for his mention of Collins in the *Essay Supplementary to the Preface* is in connection with the "Elegy," though Wordsworth does not take the occasion to say anything about Collins' poetry. As a matter of fact, the only direct judgment Wordsworth makes of Collins' poetry is in a letter to Dyce, when he says, "These three writers, Thomson, Collins, and Dyer had more poetic imagination than any of their contemporaries, unless we reckon Chatterton of that age. I do not name Pope, for he stands alone, as a man most highly gifted; but unluckily he took the plain, when the heights were within his reach." [15] The compliment to Collins is not excessive; and, in view of it, I think we need not worry about the various parallels to Collins which may ingeniously be discovered in Wordsworth's poetry.

With Coleridge the case is a little clearer. I have already quoted his comparison of Collins with Gray. In another place he expresses real enthusiasm for the "Ode on the Poetical Character":

. . . poetry, though treating on lofty and abstract truths, ought to be deemed *impassioned* by him who reads it with impassioned feelings. Now Collins's "Ode on the Poetical Character,"—that part of it, I should say, beginning with "The band (as faery legends say) Was wove on that creating day,"—has inspired and whirled *me* along with greater agitations of enthusiasm than any the most *impassioned* scene in Schiller or Shakespeare, using "impassioned" in its confined sense, for writing in which the human passions of pity, fear, anger, revenge, jealousy, or love are brought into view with their workings.[16]

In the Preface to the Second Edition Coleridge further remarks:

A poem that abounds in allusions, like the 'Bard' of Gray, or one that impersonates high and abstract truths, like Collins's 'Ode on the Poetical Character,' claims not to be popular—but should be acquitted of obscurity. The deficiency is in the Reader. But this is a charge which every poet, whose imagination is warm and rapid, must expect from his *contemporaries*. Milton did not escape it; and it was adduced with virulence against Gray and Collins. We now hear no more of it: not that their poems are better understood at present than they were at their first publication; but their fame is established; and a critic would accuse himself of frigidity or inattention who should profess not to understand them.[17]

There is no reason to think that Wordsworth's poetry would have been any different had he not read Collins; Coleridge's poetry might have been ever so slightly different had he not read the *Odes*. This statement is hard to prove, and I am not sure parallel passages prove it. There is, however, something in the personifications and in the imagery—in the tone—of certain of Coleridge's early poems which makes me think of Collins, though whether it would not make me think of Gray or Akenside were I more conscious of those poets is hard to say. The fact is that, though lines like

> When Evening's dusky car
> Crowned with her dewy star
> Steals o'er the fading sky in shadowy flight

from "Songs of the Pixies" makes us think of "Ode to Evening" (the juxtaposition of so many of Collins' words would hardly seem to be mere accident), the car of evening and anything "dewy" were part of the vocabulary of eighteenth-century verse; and likewise the similarities in personification merely point up the fact that in his early years Coleridge was only a rather advanced eighteenth-century poet. I think it very likely that Coleridge was influenced by Collins, for he obviously had read and, by his own statement, was moved by Collins' poems; but I would feel much more secure, in the case of Coleridge, in trying to show the ways in which eighteenth-century poetic forms and conventions found their home in his poetry than I would feel in attempting to demonstrate the specific influence of any particular eighteenth-century poet.

With Keats the problem of the possible influence of Collins is more interesting, much more challenging, and probably impossibly vague. It seems to me that Keats was by all odds the greatest poet among the "Romantics," and therefore I would most happily show that Collins influenced Keats. Unfortunately for this exercise, Keats names Collins only once, in a letter in which he says he heard Hazlitt's lecture mentioning Collins, and he does not comment on the lecture. Surely no one could say that Keats was very conscious of Collins' influence, and should we start talking of unconscious influences we would enter dangerous shoals indeed. However, we know from Leigh Hunt's *Autobiography* that this mentor of Keats was in his early years "passionately in love with Collins and Gray";[18] and, since one usually attempts to convert others, even in maturity, to one's own youthful passions, there seems a good likelihood that, if Keats did not himself discover Collins, Leigh Hunt introduced his young friend to his own early enthusiasm.

Not that such a line of argument takes us very far. It is some-what more helpful that Mr. Ainsworth cites ten or a dozen parallel passages in which the verbal resemblances between Keats and Collins are near enough to make us wonder whether Keats might just possibly have been remembering, willfully or not, his pred-ecessor. More interestingly, several scholars have pointed out a clear resemblance between "To Autumn" and "Ode to Eve-ning," [19] the sort of resemblance which a fairly sensitive reader can feel without being able to say exactly wherein it consists. The resemblance lies in the manner of proceeding in the poem. Col-lins and Keats handle their respective goddesses in much the same way; the two divinities share a family likeness in that the qualities of the season autumn are attributed to the presiding spirit, Autumn, in the same way as Evening, the personification, gathers to herself the enchantments of the time of day she repre-sents. Is this evidence of an "influence"? Hardly, in any literal sense; it is evidence only that the two poets met a challenge of their craft in the same way, and evidence that Keats was more influenced in general by eighteenth-century conventions then he himself admitted. Yet we are justified in wondering not alto-gether idly whether Keats would have written "To Autumn" in just the way he did had Collins not written first.

But the question may be reduced more specifically to one of form. Professor George N. Shuster, in his study of the English ode, remarks:

When . . . the question is asked as to what Keats's place in the history of the form may be, the historian must inevitably turn to Collins as a basis for comparison. For the great odes of 1819 are more perfect appli-cations of the norm established by the "Popular Superstitions" ode. Keats shortened the seventeen-line stanza. But above all he carried the liberation of the form from expressionism, whether artificial or spon-taneous, a full step farther. Like Collins he was not concerned primarily with the statement of an idea or the utterance of emotion, but with the creation of an image which, fringed with kindred lesser images, would then suggest the poet's mood and thought.[20]

This is probably as far as we dare go in suggesting an influence, and it may not seem very far. Yet, if it be true that Collins did indeed begin something which Keats brought to the glorious perfection of his odes, surely nothing more need be said to suggest the importance of Collins' influence on later poets.

V *Appraisal*

It is now time to return to the question I raised at the beginning of this chapter: "How good is Collins' poetry?"—or rather, as I should prefer to phrase it, "How good is Collins as a poet?" I have already adumbrated the answer through various digressions. We have seen some of the sources of Collins' poetry, said something about his fame, and examined his possible influence on several poetical successors—all of which serves to place him securely within the permanent body of literature in English. It may not be entirely too much to assert that in some very tiny way our literature since 1800 would have been different had Collins not written. His small, shady place in literary history is not apt to be disturbed.

But this may be said of many poets whom I would not consider the equal of Collins. The important thing about Collins is not so much related to his place in literary history—to the faint tinge of personal color he may have cast on the literature which followed him, nor even to the degree to which he developed the technical resources at his command—as to the uniqueness of the vision which he used those technical resources to convey. There is no other writer whose works, taken as a whole, are like Collins'; and this fact alone gives him a special place. He is not like Gray at all, certainly not like Thomson, the poets with whom he is ordinarily discussed. He is quite unlike any poet who followed him; and, although he borrows freely, his own personality makes his works totally different from those from which he borrowed. He could not have accomplished such perfections as he achieved without his highly developed technique, and I have already suggested that it is the combination of technique and clarity and intensity of vision which makes a poet. These Collins had. But what is finally important about Collins is the fact that, like the very greatest poets (and I am not saying that Collins is among them—only that he shares with them this one attribute of greatness), he saw the world in a way which nobody had ever quite seen it before and has never quite seen it since, and left us a record of this vision.

The question as to whether he is a *good* poet is of the same sort as, "Is this a good dinner?" It is partly a matter of taste, and persons whose tastes have been formed in a certain way will love neither Oriental cooking nor the individual flavor of Collins' poetry. Lovers of exotic foods and Collins will inevitably feel that persons who do not share their tastes are missing exquisite if minor pleasures, but we must realize, sadly, that conversion is usually hopeless. But it is possible to say, "This would be an excellent dinner—if I liked Chinese cooking," and I hope I have been able to indicate that persons deficient in poetic sensibility of the sort required may still say, "Collins' poetry is excellent in its kind, though it is not my favorite kind."

To this limitation I must except "Ode to Evening," "How Sleep the Brave," and possibly the elegy on Thomson. I cannot imagine that anyone who professes an interest in poetry could not recognize these lyrics as belonging among the very greatest in English. Many of the other poems are indeed oddly flavored and perhaps require a specially developed taste—but these greatest of Collins' poems are direct and universal in quite the same way as the greatest of Keats' or Shakespeare's lyrics. That Collins did not write thus more often is all we need lament about his poetry. That he wrote thus twice may be enough.

Notes and References

Chapter One

1. *Gentleman's Magazine*, LI (January, 1781), 11. Moy Thomas in his edition of Collins (London, 1858) states that he saw this letter in Gilbert White's handwriting, and it has been attributed to White ever since. The attribution is likely on other grounds, since White was well acquainted with Collins.

2. *Lectures on the English Poets* (Everyman ed.) 1955, p. 115.

3. At least by the standards of his time. I shall briefly discuss the question of Collins' illness later in this chapter.

4. *The Poetical Calendar. Containing A Collection of scarce and valuable Pieces of Poetry. With Variety of Originals and Translations.* . . . By Francis Fawkes, M.A. And William Woty. . . . 1763 [vols. 11 and 12].

5. Edinburgh, 1781.

6. Samuel Johnson, "Life of Collins," *The Works of Samuel Johnson,* 1825, IV, 322. Hereafter cited as "Johnson's 'Life'."

7. The chief source for my information on Collins' life is the excellent series of articles by P. L. Carver, "Notes on the Life of Collins," *Notes and Queries*, CLXXVII (August 19 and 26, September 2, 9, 16, 23, and 30, and October 7 and 14, 1939). Very little has been added to our knowledge of Collins' life since Carver wrote, and it is very likely that Mr. Carver exhausted the possibilities now known for acquiring new information. I make this general and grateful acknowledgment of indebtedness to Carver's work, which provides exhaustive documentation. I must remark, however, that I have occasionally been somewhat bolder in my interpretations than Carver has been. I shall hereafter cite Carver's series of articles simply as "Carver" with a page number. The volume of *Notes and Queries* is paginated continuously.

8. James Dallaway, *A History of the Western Division of the County of Sussex, including the Rapes of Chichester, Arundel and Bramber* . . . (London, 1815), I, part i, 208.

9. He is so called in the will of William Payne, his brother-in-law,

dated 1720, but the distinction between a hatter and a haberdasher does not seem to have been very distinct.

10. Carver, p. 146.

11. Dallaway, *ibid.*, p. 145.

12. See Carver's whole article for August 19, 1939.

13. *The Poetical Works of William Collins* (ed. with memoir by W. Moy Thomas), Aldine Edition (London, 1858), p. x.

14. *Ibid.*, p. xi.

15. H. W. Garrod devotes the first chapter of his *Collins* (Oxford, 1928) to this task. Garrod's book, however, is not easy to come by, and in certain respects my interpretations differ rather widely from his, hence I do not hesitate to repeat, in small part, his work. Anyone who is seriously interested in Collins must read Garrod's chapter.

16. *Poems on Several Occasions,* By the Reverend Mr. Thomas Warton, Batchelor of Divinity, Late Vicar of *Basing stoke* in *Hampshire,* and sometime Professor of Poetry in the University of Oxford (London, 1748), pp. 116-17.

17. *The Crypt,* II (Jan. 1, 1828), pp. 56-58. There are only three volumes of this publication, which was devoted to Hampshire antiquities and Wykehamical curiosities. See also Carver, p. 272.

18. See A. D. McKillop, "A Poem in the Collins Canon," *MLN,* XXXVII (1922), p. 181; E. R. Wasserman, "A Doubtful Poem in the Collins Canon," *MLN,* LIV (1939), pp. 361-62; Carver, p. 272; E. R. Wasserman, "Collins's 'Young Damon of the vale is dead,' " *Notes and Queries,* CLXXVIII (1940), pp. 193-94; P. L. Carver, "Collins's 'Young Damon'," *Notes and Queries,* CLXXX (1941), pp. 407-08. The arguments are inconclusive. Mr. Carver, in rejecting Collins' authorship, must, it seems to me, considerably strain the interpretation of the note which accompanied the first publication of the poem, and he too easily disregards the acceptance of the poem into the collection of 1790, at a time when, if even the most cursory editorial criticism was employed (which, of course, may not have been the case), the means for arriving at a decision in favor of inclusion were somewhat more easily come by than in 1940.

19. John Wooll, *Biographical Memoirs of the late Rev⁴ Joseph Warton, D.D.* (London, 1806), p. 107, p. 109.

20. On p. 4 Wooll attributes the puff to Johnson.

21. J. M. Murry, "The Poetry of William Collins," *Countries of the Mind,* London, 1922), p. 84.

22. *Poetical Works,* with the life of the author by Dr. Johnson; observations on his writings by Dr. Langhorne; and biographical and critical notes, by the Rev. Alexander Dyce, A.B. Oxon. (London, 1827), p. 10. Hereafter cited as "Dyce."

23. Review of Garrod's *Collins, Review of English Studies,* VI (1930), p. 237.

24. See, in addition to Carver, John R. Bloxam, *A Register of . . . Members of Saint Mary Magdalen College . . .* VI (Oxford and London, 1879), pp. 254-55.

25. *The Poetical Works of Mr. William Collins,* With Memoirs of the Author . . . by J. Langhorne (London, New Ed., 1781), pp. vi-vii.

26. Edward Gibbon, *Memoirs . . . ,* ed. G. B. Hill (London, 1900), pp. 50-52, p. 57.

27. Dyce, p. 22.

28. See, for example, Oswald Doughty, *The English Lyric in the Age of Reason* (London, 1922), p. 142: "So Collins, the poet of Fancy, of romantic imagination and classic calm, foresakes academic theory for the burning, passionate experience of active Life, of Man and Nature. And in the presence of that experience, classic calm inevitably disintegrates." See also Georg Himmler, "William Collins' Gedichte," *Giessener Beiträge,* Bd. II, Hft. 1 (1924), pp. 1-28.

29. Ragsdale's letter to Hymers was printed first, along with Thomas Warton's letter to Hymers, in "The Reaper," a series of essays which appeared in *The York Chronicle.* "The Reaper" was later printed as a volume, though not published. It is now excessively rare; the British Museum does not possess a copy of either publication. Ragsdale's letter was reprinted in *The Monthly Magazine,* XXI (July, 1806), p. 494, and in *The Gleaner,* ed. Nathan Drake IV (London, 1811), pp. 475-84. The two accessible printings vary from one another somewhat in detail but in no important respect. I follow Dyce's reprinting of the version in *The Monthly Magazine,* Dyce, pp. 25-26.

30. Carver, p. 147.

31. *Gentleman's Magazine,* XCIII, part ii (October, 1823), p. 334. William Payne may well have expected a sort of deference which Collins was unwilling to give. I have already mentioned that he was Collins' cousin, not his uncle; but the twenty years' difference in their ages would have made the latter relationship appear more probable. *Alumni Oxonienses* (London, 1888), reports of him: "Payne, William. s. William, of Midhurst, Sussex, gent. MAGDALEN COLL., matric. 21 Feb. 1727-8, aged 18; clerk 1728-33, B.A. 1731, chaplain 1733, fellow 1733-53, M.A. 1734, B.D. 1744, D.D. 1745, junior dean of arts 1744, bursar, 1745, vicar of Findon, Sussex, 1751, until his death in May, 1772."

32. Johnson's "Life," pp. 321-323. Part of this "Life" was published in Fawkes and Woty's *Poetical Calendar* eighteen or nineteen years after Collins' arrival in London.

33. Dyce, 22. See also H. O. White, "William Collins and Miss

Bundy," *Review of English Studies* VI (1930), pp. 437-42. Kings-square-court has now vanished entirely.

34. Dyce, 26. Ragsdale, at the point where I have inserted the ellipsis, refers to "Colonel Martyn" as the source of the money Payne distributed. We now know this to be mistaken.

35. R. Holt-White, *Letters of J. Mulso to Gilbert White* (London, 1907), p. 3. Cited hereafter as "Mulso." See Carver, pp. 168-69.

36. Charles Lennox, Earl of March, *A Duke and His Friends* (London, 1911), vol. II, pp. 456-57. See also Carver, pp. 149-50.

37. Alexander Hay, *The History of Chichester* (Chichester, 1804), p. 527.

38. Charles Lennox, Earl of March, *op. cit.*, p. 724.

39. Colton, *Hypocrisy* (1812), p. 25. Quoted from the *Dictionary of National Biography* article on Hardham. Hardham is still remembered as a benefactor of Chichester, for he left his fortune of over twenty thousand pounds for the benefit of his native city.

40. Dyce, pp. 27-28.

41. Mulso, p. 7.

42. H. O. White, "The Letters of William Collins," *Review of English Studies,* III (1927), p. 16.

43. Carver, p. 171.

44. Johnson's "Life," p. 322.

45. Charles Lennox, Earl of March, *op. cit.*, pp. 523-24, p. 511. See also Carver, p. 242.

46. Carver, p. 171.

47. Johnson's "Life," p. 322.

48. Dyce, p. 27.

49. Basil Williams, *The Whig Supremacy* (Oxford, 1939), p. 240.

50. On the apathy of the public on this occasion see W. E. H. Lecky, *A History of England in the Eighteenth Century* (London, 1920), II, p. 87.

51. Mulso, p. 9.

52. Carver, p. 185.

53. Mulso, p. 14.

54. Audrey Jennings, "William Collins's House in Chichester," *Notes and Queries,* CXCIX (February, 1954), pp. 58-60.

55. Carver, 201. See also H. O. White, "William Collins and Miss Bundy," pp. 437-42.

56. The letter has been reprinted in virtually every edition of Collins or work about him since Wooll printed it in 1806. See Wooll, p. 14; Dyce, pp. 15-16; Carver, p. 203.

57. Carver, p. 204. See also the very interesting, but admittedly highly speculative, article by Carver, "Collins and Alexander Carlyle,"

Review of English Studies, XV (January, 1939), pp. 35-44. I shall have more occasion to refer to this study in discussing several of Collins' poems.

58. Mulso, p. 15.

59. I have taken this line of argument at least partly on the basis of the tone which seems to be conveyed by Mulso's letter. I grant, however, that communications were bad; that it is conceivable that Collins did not know or bother to find out where his uncle's regiment was, or that he was simply told, if he inquired, that it was next definitely to be found in Flanders; and that it was at that time certainly easier to travel from London to Antwerp than from London to Fifeshire. Even granting this, however, I do not see it any more probable that Collins was making an expensive journey in order to ask money of an uncle who did not have much. One may desire to see one's uncle without necessarily expecting money from him.

60. *Gentleman's Magazine*, XVI (1746), p. 672.

61. Frederick Page, "An Essay by Collins," *Times Literary Supplement*, July 11, 1935, p. 448. See also E. W. H. Meyerstein, *Times Literary Supplement*, July 25 (1935), p. 477, and Carver, pp. 240-41.

62. See Carver, p. 132, and W. L. Wilmshurst, *Times Literary Supplement* (February 9, 1933), p. 92. I have not discovered what became of the documents advertised by Mr. Wilmshurst.

63. *The Poems of William Collins*, ed. W. C. Bronson (London, Ginn & Co., 1898), xxiii.

64. Dyce, p. 29.

65. [Robert Dodsley], *The Preceptor*, 1748, xxiii.

66. James Thomson, *Poetical Works*, ed. with a "Life of James Thomson" by Patrick Murdoch, 1784, I, xxiii.

67. Langhorne's edition, xi-xii.

68. S. T. Coleridge, *Specimens of the Table Talk*, 3rd ed., 1851, pp. 270-271.

69. See A. D. McKillop, "A Lost Poem by Collins," *Times Literary Supplement*, December 6, 1928.

70. Dyce, pp. 16-17.

71. See H. O. White, "The Letters of William Collins," *Review of English Studies*, III (January, 1927), pp. 19-21.

72. Johnson's "Life," p. 323.

73. Dyce, pp. 29-30.

74. Dyce, p. 22.

75. Johnson's "Life," p. 324.

76. Dyce, p. 31.

77. *Poems, with . . . Essay* by Sir Egerton Brydges (London, 1830), lxix.

78. Dyce, pp. 31-32.

79. Johnson's "Life," p. 323.

80. Dyce, pp. 23-24. The concluding quotation is from Horace, *Satires*, I, iv, 62.

Chapter Two

1. "Dialogue on Taste," *The Investigator*, 1762, pp. 63-65. A separate title page to the "Dialogue on Taste" calls it the second edition, but I am unable to find any confirmation of the publication of a first edition.

2. See Thomas Warton's edition of Milton's Minor Poems, 1785.

3. *Poems*, ed. James Kinsley (Oxford, 1958), II, p. 913.

4. *The Works of Virgil . . . The Eclogues and Georgics* [translated], with Notes on the Whole, by the Rev. Mr. Joseph Warton . . . 1753, I, iv-viii.

5. For such a history—an admirable one—consult George N. Shuster, *The English Ode from Milton to Keats* (New York, Columbia University Press, 1940).

6. *Letters Concerning Taste*, 3rd ed., 1757, p. 28. The first edition was published in 1755.

7. *An Essay on Original Genius* . . . , 1767, pp. 168, 171.

8. Every student of eighteenth-century English literature must know Samuel H. Monk's *The Sublime* (New York, 1935), now available in a paperback edition. R. S. Crane's brief review of Monk's book in *Philological Quarterly*, XV (April, 1936), pp. 165-67 should also be consulted.

9. James Beattie, "Illustrations on Sublimity," *Dissertations Moral and Critical*, 1783, pp. 620-621.

10. *Poetical Works*, ed. E. de Selincourt, 1952, II, 517.

11. Three most valuable studies of personification in eighteenth-century poetry are: Bertrand H. Bronson, "Personification Reconsidered," *E.L.H.*, XIV (1947), pp. 163-177; Rachel Trickett, "The Augustan Pantheon: Mythology and Personification in Eighteenth-Century Poetry," *Essays and Studies Collected for the English Association*, vi (1953), pp. 71-86; and Earl R. Wasserman, "The Inherent Values of 18th Century Personification," *PMLA*, LXV (June 1950), pp. 435-463.

12. John Ogilvie, *Poems on Several Subjects* . . . , 1762, lx-lxi, lxii, lxiii-lxiv. The emphases are Ogilvie's own.

13. *The Adventurer*, 57 (May 22, 1753).

14. *Works of Virgil*, iii.

15. 3rd ed., 1757.

16. For a development of this point and a stunning defense of per-

sonification, to which my remarks are much indebted, see Professor Bronson's article cited above.

17. 1748, I, pp. 358-59.

18. [Henry Pemberton], *Observations on Poetry* . . . , 1738, p. 92.

19. *An Essay on Mr. Pope's Odyssey. In Five Dialogues* . . . , 2nd ed., 1737, pp. 224-25.

20. "The Natural History of Religion," *Four Dissertations,* 1757, pp. 5, 17, 18.

21. "Inherent Values . . . ," pp. 438-440.

22. *An Essay on Original Genius,* pp. 176-77.

23. Geoffrey Tillotson, "Eighteenth-Century Poetic Diction," *Essays and Studies by Members of the English Association,* XXV (1939) (Oxford, 1940), p. 65.

24. John Arthos, *The Language of Natural Description in Eighteenth-Century Poetry,* Ann Arbor, University of Michigan Press (University of Michigan Publications, Language and Literature, XXIV), 1949, pp. 393-404.

25. F. W. Bateson, *English Poetry and the English Language* (Oxford, 1934), pp. 69-70.

26. *Ibid.,* pp. 65-66. My remarks on diction are much indebted to Professor Bateson's chapter on the Augustans, as they are to Professor Tillotson's essay cited above.

27. *Correspondence of Gray, Walpole, West, and Ashton,* ed. Paget Toynbee, 1915, II, 27.

28. See Josephine Miles, *The Primary Language of Poetry in the 1740's and 1840's,* Berkeley and Los Angeles, University of California Press (University of California Publications in English, XIX, 2), 1950; especially, for Collins, pp. 189-94.

29. *Works of Virgil,* iv-v.

30. Beattie, *op. cit.,* pp. 647-651.

31. Johnson's "Life," p. 324.

Chapter Three

1. *Works,* 1908, III, 508.

2. See Edward Gay Ainsworth, Jr., *Poor Collins,* Ithaca, N.Y., 1937, pp. 154-57.

3. *Works of Alexander Pope,* ed. J. Warton 1797, I, pp. 61-62.

4. *The Poems of William Collins,* ed. W. C. Bronson, 1898, xliii.

5. [Thomas] Salmon, *Modern History: or the Present State of all Nations* . . . 1744, I, 337. The chapter on Persia extends through pp. 305-382.

6. J. W. Mackail, "Collins and the English Lyric in the Eighteenth Century," *Essays by Divers Hands,* Transactions of the Royal Society

of Literature of the United Kingdom, N.S. I, 1921, p. 9. The essay is reprinted in Mackail's *Studies of English Poets* (New York, 1926), pp. 137-158.

7. William Collins, *Drafts & Fragments of Verse,* ed. J. S. Cunningham (Oxford, 1956). For epistolary fragments see 19-30.

8. *Ibid.,* Frag. 8, lines 13-18, pp. 23-24. Monimia is the heroine of *The Orphan* by Otway. *Cf.* Collins' praises for Otway in "Ode to Pity."

9. See Ainsworth, pp. 180-82.

10. *Poems,* 1898, p. 82.

11. The volume is dated 1747 on the title page, but it was published in December, 1746.

12. H. W. Garrod, *Collins* (Oxford, 1928), p. 45.

13. S. Musgrove, "The Theme of Collins's Odes," *Notes and Queries,* CLXXXV (1943), pp. 214-217.

14. Pp. 69-70; 78.

15. Letter to Hymers, reprinted in *The Gleaner,* ed. Nathan Drake, CLXXXVII (1811), p. 478.

16. Collins was undoubtedly aware that, if he were genuinely copying Greek forms, the epode should follow the strophe and antistrophe. We may argue with his nomenclature or with his scholarship, but not with the form of his finished poems.

17. *The Poetical Works of Mr. William Collins* with a prefatory essay by Mrs. Barbauld, 1797, xxii.

18. See Raymond D. Havens, "Simplicity. A Changing Concept," *Journal of the History of Ideas,* XIV (January, 1953), pp. 3-32.

19. *The Poetical Works* . . . Essay on the Genius and Writings of Collins by Sir Egerton Brydges, Bart., 1830, xlviii.

20. Langhorne's edition, p. 158.

21. Robert A. Anderson, *A Complete Edition of the Poets of Great Britain,* 1794, IX, p. 516. Anderson slightly misquotes the *Monthly Review,* XXX (January, 1764), p. 24.

22. For an interesting speculation on the situation surrounding the composition of this ode as well as "Ode to Evening" and "Colonel Ross" see P. L. Carver's "Collins and Alexnder Carlyle," *Review of English Studies,* XV (January, 1939), pp. 35-44.

23. Carver, pp. 220-22.

24. Lecky, *A History of England in the Eighteenth Century,* 1920, II, p. 30.

25. See W. C. Bronson's edition, pp. 105-06.

26. Ainsworth, p. 75.

27. See Thomas Warton's *History of English Poetry,* 1774, Vol. I, Dissertation I, "Of the Origin of Romantic Fiction in Europe."

The pages of the two prefatory Dissertations are unnumbered, but the particular passage, and footnote "g," occurs on the 4th and 5th pages following f2. See also J. M. S. Tompkins, "In Yonder Grave a Druid Lies," *Review of English Studies*, XXII (1946), pp. 1-16. Also of great interest is a passage from Martin Martin's *A Description of the Western Isles of Scotland Circa 1695*, 1703, 1716 (Stirling, Eneas Mackay, 1934), pp. 167-68, which we know from "Ode on the Popular Superstitions . . ." that Collins read, though he may not have read it when he wrote "Ode to Liberty": "Before they engaged the enemy in battle, the chief Druid harangued the army to excite their courage. He was placed on an eminence, from whence he addressed himself to all of them standing about him, putting them in mind of what great things were performed by the valour of their ancestors, raised their hopes with the noble rewards of honour and victory, and dispelled their fears by all the topics that a natural courage could suggest. After this harangue, the army gave a general shout, and then charged the enemy stoutly."

28. *Countries of the Mind*, 1922, p. 91.

29. Ainsworth, pp. 148-53; pp. 193-97. For another very illuminating discussion of the ode see A. S. P. Woodhouse, "Collins and the Creative Imagination," *Studies in English by Members of the University College, Toronto* (Toronto, 1931), pp. 113-19.

30. See Garrod, pp. 84-85.

31. *Drafts and Fragments*, pp. 10-13.

32. The stanza has been quite widely imitated. See the review of Garrod, *Times Literary Supplement*, February 7, 1929, p. 95; Ronald Bailey, *Times Literary Supplement*, April 11, 1929, p. 295; H. O. White, *Times Literary Supplement*, April 18, 1929, p. 315; and R. D. Havens, *The Influence of Milton on English Poetry*, 1922, pp. 561, 565.

33. See Garrod, pp. 48-50; J. R. MacPhail, *Times Literary Supplement*, March 22, 1928; Margaret Bourke, *Times Literary Supplement*, March 29, 1928; and John Sparrow, *Times Literary Supplement*, April 12, 1928.

34. Langhorne's edition, p. 181.

35. "Philo-Lyristes" in *Gentleman's Magazine*, LII (1782), p. 22.

36. *Great Expectations*, 3rd ed., 1861, I, p. 91.

37. See Chapter I, p. 51.

38. Musgrove, "The Theme of Collins's Odes," p. 215.

39. *Ibid.*, p. 255.

40. J. M. S. Tompkins, "In Yonder Grave . . ." 1-6; E. M. W. Tillyard, "William Collins's 'Ode on the Death of Thomson'," *Review of English Literature*, I (July, 1960), pp. 30-38. I am much indebted

to these two articles, particularly to the latter in my discussion of the poem.

41. Johnson's "Life," p. 324.

42. Royal Society of Edinburgh, *Transactions*, I (1788), "Papers of the Literary Class," 65.

43. W. C. Bronson's edition, pp. 121-32. See also Ainsworth, pp. 322-23.

44. Henry A. Beers, *A History of English Romanticism in the Eighteenth Century* (New York, 1899), p. 114.

45. 1716, pp. 300-35.

46. *Ibid.*, pp. 260-61. For a most illuminating discussion of Collins' use of another book by Martin, *A Late Voyage to St. Kilda* (1698), see A. S. P. Woodhouse, "Collins and Martin Martin," *Times Literary Supplement* (December 20, 1928, *et seq.*).

Chapter Four

1. *Countries of the Mind*, p. 83.

2. Woodhouse, "Collins and the Creative Imagination," p. 62.

3. H. O. White, "Letters of William Collins," *Review of English Studies*, III (January, 1927), p. 14.

4. "The 'Morceau de fantasie' in Verse: A New Approach to Collins," *University of Toronto Quarterly*, XV (1945), pp. 65-69.

5. Woodhouse's whole essay (Toronto, 1931) is relevant here.

6. The whole second section of *Poor Collins* is devoted to this matter. See Ainsworth, pp. 119-217.

7. *Classical Influences on English Poetry*, 1951, p. 150.

8. See Oswald Doughty, *The English Lyric in the Age of Reason*, 1922, p. 97.

9. *Gentleman's Magazine*, LII (1782), pp. 20-21.

10. Edith Morely (ed.), *The Correspondence of Henry Crabb Robinson with the Wordsworth Circle* . . . (Oxford, 1927), I, p. 45.

11. *Coleridge the Talker* (ed. Richard W. Armour and Raymond F. Howes) (London, 1940), p. 159.

12. *English Poets* (ed. Humphrey Ward), 1880, III, p. 279.

13. Gray, *Correspondence* (ed. Paget Toynbee and Leonard Whibley), Oxford, 1935, I, p. 261.

14. Mr. Ainsworth, with his usual thoroughness, has collected the data on "The Rise of Collins's Literary Reputation" in *Poor Collins*, pp. 222-43. The earliest critical notice of Collins after Johnson's essay in the *Poetical Calendar* appeared in *The Monthly Review*, XXX (January, 1764), p. 26, which concludes: "It is with peculiar pleasure that we do this justice to a Poet who was too great to be popular, and whose genius was neglected, because it was above the common taste." See

also A. S. P. Woodhouse, "Collins in the Eighteenth Century," *Times Literary Supplement* (October 16, 1930).

15. *Letters of the Wordsworth Family* (ed. W. Knight) (Boston, 1907), II, p. 359. The letter is dated January 12, 1829.

16. *Letters* (ed. E. H. Coleridge), 1895, I, pp. 196-97.

17. *The Poetical Works of Samuel Taylor Coleridge* (ed. James Dykes Campbell), 1925, p. 540.

18. Ed. Roger Ingpen, 1903, I, p. 86. See also pp. 88 and 92.

19. Ainsworth, p. 276; W. C. Bronson's edition, xlviii; Edmund Blunden, *Nature in English Literature*, 1929, pp. 44-47.

20. Shuster, pp. 268-69. See also p. 270.

Selected Bibliography

The first section of the following bibliography is a list of the editions and printings of Collins' works. It makes no pretense to be exhaustive, but I have included many items of no scholarly importance in order to demonstrate the continuity of Collins' fame. An asterisk marks those editions of textual importance. The second section, also selective, lists the most significant studies having a bearing on Collins. It is to be noted that the important biographical materials are gathered together in Dyce's edition of the poems, and that W. C. Bronson's edition includes important critical material.

PRIMARY SOURCES

Editions of Collins' Poems & Prose

*Persian Eclogues. London, Roberts, 1742.

*Verses humbly address'd to Sir Thomas Hanmer on his edition of Shakespeare's Works, by a Gentleman of Oxford. London: Cooper, 1743. Price Six Pence.

*An Epistle: addrest to Sir Thomas Hanmer, on his Edition of Shakespear's Works. The Second Edition. To which is added, A Song from the Cymbelyne of the same Author. By Mr. William Collins, of Magdalene-College in Oxford. London: Dodsley and Cooper, 1744. Price One Shilling.

The Museum: or, the Literary and Historical Register. London: Printed for R. Dodsley, in Pall Mall, 1746. [Number VI, June 7, contains the "Ode to a Lady."]

*Odes on several Descriptive and Allegoric Subjects, by William Collins. London: Millar, 1747. [This volume actually appeared in December 1746.]

*A Collection of Poems. By Several Hands. In Three Volumes. London. Printed for R. Dodsley. Second Edition, 1748. [This second edition contains in Vol. I the "Ode to a Lady," "Ode to Evening," and "How Sleep the Brave." Vol. IV, 1755, added "Epistle to Hanmer" and "A Song from . . . Cymbeline." Important for variants in

"Ode to Evening." The *Collection* was reprinted in 1763, 1765, 1767, 1783.]

*An *Ode occasion'd by the death of Mr. Thomson*, by William Collins. London: Manby, 1749.

The Passions, an Ode. Winchester. [1750] [A version with the last twenty-four lines rewritten by the Earl of Lichfield for Dr. Hayes' musical setting.]

The Passions, an Ode. Written by Mr. Collins. Set to Musick by Dr. Hayes. Performed at the Theatre in Oxford, July 2, 1750. [Also with the Earl of Lichfield's revisions.]

The Union: or, Select Scots and English Poems. Edinburgh, 1753. [Includes "Ode to Evening" and "Ode on the Death of Mr. Thomson."]

Oriental Eclogues. London: Payne, 1757. Price one Shilling.

The Poetical Calendar. Written and selected by Francis Fawkes, M.A., and William Woty. 1763. [Vol. xi, November, contains the "Oriental Eclogues," the twelve Odes, "Epistle to Sir Thomas Hanmer," and "A Song from . . . Cymbeline." Vol. xii added the "Ode on the Death of Mr. Thomson" and Johnson's memoir.]

The Poetical Works of Mr. William Collins, with Memoirs of the Author; and Observations on his genius and writings, by J. Langhorne. London, Becket and Dehondt, 1765. [Contains all poems except "Popular Superstitions," "Verses Written on a Paper," "To Miss Aurelia C————r," "Sonnet," and "Song (Damon)." Established the text until Bronson's edition of 1898. Reprinted in 1771 (according to Dyce), 1776, 1781.]

Beauties of English Poesy, Selected by Oliver Goldsmith. London: William Griffin, 1767. ["Oriental Eclogues" appear in Vol. I, pp. 239-253.]

Poems for Young Ladies [edited by Oliver Goldsmith]. [London] 1767. ["Oriental Eclogues" appear on pp. 228-41. This volume was republished in 1770 and 1785.]

Poetical Works of Mr. William Collins. To Which are added Mr. Hammond's Elegies. Glasgow: Foulis, 1770. [Foulis' edition was reprinted by Balfour and Creech of Edinburgh as Volume XLIII in the *British Poets*.]

The Works of the English Poets. With Prefaces, Biographical and Critical, by Samuel Johnson. Volume the Forty Ninth. London: J. Nichols . . . 1779. [Reprinted, 1790 adding the "Song (Young Damon)" to the collected works. The song had appeared in the *Gentleman's Magazine* for February, 1788.]

The Poetical Works of William Collins. With the Life of the Author.

Edinburgh: Apollo Press, 1781. [Langhorne's "Life." Vol. LXXX-VIII of Bell's *Poets of Great Britain*. Reprinted 1787.]

The Poetical Works of William Collins. Glasgow: Andrew Foulis, 1787. Folio. [Derived from Langhorne. Unauthoritative variants in "Ode to a Lady" and "Ode to Evening."]

°Transactions of the Royal Society of Edinburgh. Volume I. Edinburgh, 1788. [Part II, *Papers of the Literary Class*, pp. 63-75, is the first publication of the "Ode on the Popular Superstitions of the Highlands. . . ."]

An *Ode on the Popular Superstitions of the Highlands of Scotland, etc.* London: Bell, 1788. [A spurious edition. This text was accepted, however, until Bronson's edition of 1898.]

The Poetical Works of William Collins . . . To which is prefixed the Life of the Author. London: J. & A. Arch; Edinburgh: Bell & Bradfute, 1794. [In Vol. IX of *A Complete Edition of the Poets of Great Britain*, ed. Robert Anderson.]

Roach's Beauties of the Poets of Great Britain . . . From the Works of the Most Admired Authors. 6 vols. London: John Roach, 1794. 12 mo. [Vol. IV contains "How Sleep the Brave," "Oriental Eclogues," "Ode on the Poetical Character."]

Poems by William Collins, being Odes descriptive and allegorical, with the Ode on the popular Superstitions of the Highlands of Scotland . . . Colchester: W. Keymer, June: 1796.

Poetical Works. With a Prefatory Essay by Mrs. Barbauld. London: Cadell and Davies, 1797. [I was unable to locate a putative 1794 edition.]

Poetical Works, enriched with elegant engravings. London: T. Bensley, for E. Harding, 1798.

Poetical Works. London: Sharpe, 1804. [Includes Langhorne's commentary and Johnson's "Life." Illustrated with engravings.]

°The Poetical Works of William Collins. Collated with the Best Editions, by Thomas Park. London: J. Sharpe, 1805. [Volume XXX of the *Works of the British Poets* edited by Park. The first attempt at a critical edition.]

°Poetical Works, with the Life of the Author by Dr. Johnson; Observations on his Writings by Dr. Langhorne; and Biographical and Critical Notes . . . by the Rev. Alexander Dyce. London: Pickering, 1827. [Dyce made no important textual criticism, but the notes are invaluable.]

The Poems of William Collins, with notes selected from the editions of Langhorne and Mrs. Barbauld, and original; together with Dr. Johnson's Life of the Author, corrected and enlarged. By the Rev.

William Crowe, Public Orator of the University of Oxford. Bath: E. Collings, 1828.

Poems, with Memoir (by Sir Harris Nicolas), and Essay by Sir Egerton Brydges. Langhorne's "Observations." London: Pickering (Aldine Poets), 1830. [Republished 1832 with a new Preface.]

The Poetical Works of . . . William Collins . . . edited (with memoir) by the Rev. Robert Aris Willmott. London: George Routledge, 1854.

Poems, with Memoir, by W. Moy Thomas. London: Pickering (Aldine Poets), 1858. [New material, dropping Brydges and Langhorne.]

Poems, edited by W. C. Bronson. London and Boston: Ginn & Co., 1898. [Demolished the spurious edition of "Popular Superstitions." Valuable notes.]

Poems, with Memoir, by Christopher Stone. London: Frowde, 1907.

Poems, edited with an Introductory Study by Edmund Blunden. London: F. Etchells & H. Macdonald (The Haslewood Books), 1929.

Poems of William Collins, edited by Christopher Stone and Austin Lane Poole. (*The Poems of Gray and Collins,* Edited by Austin Lane Poole.) London, New York, Toronto: Oxford University Press, 1936. [The 1936 edition of this standard volume incorporated the latest textual criticism of Collins by Garrod and others.]

SECONDARY SOURCES

AINSWORTH, EDWARD GAY, JR. *Poor Collins.* Ithaca, N.Y.: Cornell University Press, 1937. Inaccurate biography; industrious, scholary criticism, approached from a point of view now outdated.

BROWN, MERLE E. "On William Collins' 'Ode to Evening,'" *Essays in Criticism,* XI (April, 1961), 136-53. A most illuminating and important essay discussing Evening as a personification.

CARVER, P. L. "Collins and Alexander Carlyle," *Review of English Studies,* XV (January, 1939), 35-44. Speculation as to genesis of "Ode to Evening" and "How Sleep the Brave."

————. "Notes on the Life of Collins," *Notes and Queries,* CLXXVII (1939). August 19 and 26; September 2, 9, 16, 23, and 30; October 7 and 14. Virtually the only significant contributions to Collins' biography since the eighteenth century. Forces a drastic revision of Johnson's "Life."

COFFMAN, GEORGE R. "Collins and Thomson," *Modern Language Notes,* XXXI (1916), 378-79. Parallels between passages in "Popular Superstitions" and "Winter."

CUNNINGHAM, J. S. "Thomas Warton and William Collins: A Footnote," *Durham University Journal,* XLVI, No. 1 (1953), 22-24. ". . . few

thoughts and enthusiasms [Joseph Warton] and Collins did not
share."

GARROD, H. W. *Collins:* Oxford: Oxford U.P. 1928. Standard work.

———. "Errors in the Text of Collins," *Times Literary Supplement,*
March 15, 1928 *et seq.* The substantive suggestions are incorporated in the last Oxford edition.

[GRAINGER, J.] Review of "Oriental Eclogues" *Monthly Review,* XVI
(1757), 486-89.

HIMMLER, GEORG. *Collins Gedichte, Giessener Beiträge* II (hft. I),
1924. Presents Collins as a "Romantic" battling neoclassic dragons.

MACKAIL, J. W. "Collins and the English Lyric in the Eighteenth Century." *Essays by Divers Hands.* Transactions of the Royal Society
of Literature of the United Kingdom, N.S. Vol. I, 1921, pp. 1-23.
(Reprinted in *Studies of English Poets* by J. W. Mackail, New
York: Longmans, Green & Co., 1926, pp. 137-58.) Perceptive and
sensitive, though based on a view of eighteenth-century poetry no
longer tenable.

MCKILLOP, ALAN D. "Collins's *Ode to Evening*—Background and
Structure," *Tennessee Studies in Literature,* V (1960), 73-83.
Sensitive interpretation.

———. "Collins's 'Ode to the Passions,'" *Times Literary Supplement,*
March 7, 1936. Concerned with the text used by Hayes in setting
the ode to music.

———. "The Romanticism of William Collins," *Studies in Philology,*
XX (1923), 1-16. Important as perhaps the earliest essay to point
out that Collins' "Romanticism" is the result of taking seriously
certain neoclassical critical commonplaces.

MEYERSTEIN, E. H. W. "Collins' Ode on Col. Ross," *Times Literary Supplement,* July 4, 1935. A misquotation of the ode in a novel of
1756.

———. "A Hitherto Unpublished Letter of William Collins," *London
Mercury,* XI (December, 1924), 169-74. The letter to John Gilbert Cooper.

MULSO, REV. JOHN. *The Letters to Gilbert White of Selborne from . . .
The Rev. John Mulso.* Ed. . . . by Rashleigh Holt-White. London, 1906. The only available text of the letters mentioning Collins.

MURRY, J. MIDDLETON. "The Poetry of William Collins," *Countries of
the Mind.* London: 1922, 81-99. The "triumphs and dangers of the
pursuit of style." A perceptive essay.

MUSGROVE, S. "The Theme of Collins's Odes," *Notes and Queries,*
CLXXXV (1943), October 9 and 23. An effort, generally successful, to provide a large context of meaning for the odes.

PAGE, FREDERICK, "An Essay by Collins," *Times Literary Supplement,* July 11, 1935. An effort to attribute to Collins an essay in Dodsley's *Museum* for July 4, 1747.

SHUSTER, GEORGE N. *The English Ode from Milton to Keats.* New York: Columbia University Press, 1940. A most sensitive and important treatment.

STONE, C. R., "Collins's 'Ode to Evening,'" *Academy,* No. 1936 (June 12, 1909), 205-6. The artistic relevance of the verbal changes.

————. "The Story of a Poem," *Academy,* No. 1805 (December 8, 1906), 587-88. Discussion of "Popular Superstitions."

SYPHER, WYLIE, "The 'Morceau de fantasie' in Verse: a new approach to Collins." *University of Toronto Quarterly,* XV (1945), 65-69. Collins as a rococo artist. A valuable insight.

TILLOTSON, GEOFFREY. "Notes on William Collins." *Essays in Criticism and Research.* London: Cambridge University Press, 1942. Collins' diction. Corrects Ainsworth at several points.

TILLYARD, E. M. W. "William Collins's 'Ode on the Death of Thomson,'" *Review of English Literature,* I (July, 1960), 30-38. Develops further several points made by Tompkins. A fine appreciation and a subtle analysis.

TOMPKINS, J. M. S. " 'In Yonder Grave a Druid Lies,'" *Review of English Studies,* XXII (1946), 1-16. Important and revealing discussion of implications of the word "druid."

VIVANTE, LEONE. "The Concept of a Creative Principle in Collins and Gray." *English Poetry and its Contribution to the Knowledge of a Creative Principle.* London: Faber and Faber, 1950. A subtle, if confused, discussion of "Simplicity" as the creative principle.

WHITE, H. O. "Collins and his Contemporary Critics," *Times Literary Supplement,* January 5, 12, 1922. Although Collins was neglected, there was more notice taken of him than had previously been thought.

————. "The Dirge in Cymbeline," *Times Literary Supplement,* February 16, 1922. Bibliographical information.

————. "The Letters of William Collins," *Review of English Studies* III (January, 1927), 12-21. Convenient source for the texts.

————. Review of H. W. Garrod's *Collins, Review of English Studies* VI (1930), 236-40. Generally approving, though correcting Garrod at several points.

————. "William Collins and Miss Bundy," *Review of English Studies* VI (1930), 437-42. Sound biographical speculation.

WOODHOUSE, A. S. P. "Collins and Martin Martin," *Times Literary Supplement,* December 20, 1928 *et seq.* Collins' use of sources for "Popular Superstitions."

Selected Bibliography

————. "Collins and the Creative Imagination," *Studies in English by Members of University College, Toronto,* Toronto, 1931, 60-129. Extremely valuable discussion of the implications of the "Ode on the Poetical Character."

————. "Collins in the Eighteenth Century," *Times Literary Supplement,* October 16, 1930. Collins' rise to fame.

Index

Addison, Joseph, 65, 71, 72; *The Spectator*, 65, 71
Aeschylus, 102
Ainsworth, Edward Gay, 93, 115, 118, 153, 159, 163
Akenside, Mark, 154, 162
Albemarle, Arnold Joost van Keppel, 1st earl of, 39
Anderson, Robert, 106
Ariosto, 58
Aristotle, 28, 32, 37, 40, 41, 43, 48, 74, 98, 100, 101, 103; *Poetics*, 32, 43, 98, 100
Arthos, John, 80

Bacon, Sir Francis, 59
Barbara Allen, 24
Barbauld, Mrs. Laetitia, 103, 136
Barrow, Thomas, 50
Bateson, F. W., 80, 81
Beattie, James, 68, 83-84; "Illustrations on Sublimity," 68, 83-84
Biographia Britannica, 35, 41
Bion, 23
Blackstone, Mr., 51
Blair, Robert, 110, 144; *The Grave*, 144
Blake, William, 135
Boswell, James, 48
Bowles, William Lisle, 159
British Magazine, 46
Bronson, W. C., 47, 89, 93, 98, 139
Brydges, Sir Egerton, 53, 106
Bundy, Miss, 33, 37, 42, 43
Burns, Robert, 135

Butcher, S. H., 43
Byron, George Gordon, Lord, 157

Caedmon, 57
Carlyle, Alexander, 138, 139
Carver, P. L., 19, 20, 31, 32, 39, 40, 167
Chatterton, Thomas, 159, 160
Chaucer, Geoffrey, 145; "Prologue" to the *Canterbury Tales*, 146
Chippendale, Thomas, 150-51
Clarke, Mr., 51
Claude of Lorraine, 127
Coleridge, Sir John Taylor, 156
Coleridge, Samuel Taylor, 49, 78, 119, 156, 157, 161-62; *Lyrical Ballads*, 135; "Songs of the Pixies," 162
A Collection of Poems . . . by Several Hands (Dodsley), 48, 95, 111, 155
Collins, Anne, 19, 40
Collins, Charles, 39, 40
Collins, Elizabeth, 19, 40
Collins, William (father), 19, 20
Collins, William (the poet),
  LIFE:
  birth and family, 18-19
  Prebendal Free School, Chichester, 19-20
  life at Winchester College, 20-21, 23
  first poems, 21-25
  influence of the Wartons, 21-23, 88
  life at Oxford, 27-28

"rebellion" and departure from Oxford, 22, 29-31

early life in London, 32-40

literary efforts in London, 35, 37, 38, 40-43, 46-51

escape to country near Richmond, 36, 40-41

trips to Flanders, 36, 41-42, 45-46, 171

illness, 17, 18, 47, 48, 52-54

death, 54

influence on the Romantic Poets, 159-64

reputation and significance, 17, 18, 155-59, 164-65

WRITINGS:

"Clarendon Review," 47

Drafts and Fragments of Verse, 105, 120, 127, 133, 150

"An Epistle to the Editor of Fairfax his Translation of Tasso's Jerusalem," 50

"The Manners. An Ode," 29-30, 99-100, 128-30, 134

"Ode Occasion'd by the Death of Mr. Thomson," 48, 49, 116, 135-138, 147, 154, 160, 165

"Ode on the Music of the Grecian Theatre," 51, 134

"Ode on the Poetical Character," 46, 98, 99, 100, 106-8, 128, 134, 148, 149, 152, 161

"Ode on the Popular Superstitions of the Highlands of Scotland, Considered as the Subject of Poetry," 48, 50, 93, 95, 138-44, 146, 151-52, 159, 163

"Ode, to a Lady on the Death of Colonel Charles Ross in the Action at Fontenoy," 42, 44, 48, 99, 110-12, 113, 118

"Ode to Evening," 21, 23, 47, 48, 57, 70, 71, 79-80, 98, 99, 100, 112, 113, 119-28, 135, 138, 145, 146, 148, 150, 154, 155, 156, 157-58, 163, 165

"Ode to Fear," 41, 69, 72, 95, 98, 99, 100, 101, 102-3, 129, 134

"Ode to Liberty," 42, 69, 99, 114-119, 142, 148, 149, 151, 153

"Ode to Mercy," 99, 112-13, 114

"Ode to Peace," 99, 100, 113-14, 118, 128, 152

"Ode to Pity," 41, 98, 99, 100, 101-2, 134

"Ode to Simplicity," 95, 98, 99, 100, 103-6, 113, 134

Odes on Several Descriptive and Allegoric Subjects, 46, 49, 62, 71, 85, 96, 100, 105, 119, 135, 138, 153, 156, 157, 161

"Of the Essential Excellencies in Poetry," 46

"On Hercules," 24, 55

"On the Battle of the Schoolbooks," 21

"The Passions. An Ode for Music," 51, 55, 87, 99, 100, 130-34, 146, 149, 150, 151

Persian Eclogues, 23, 26, 27, 31, 87, 89-94, 98, 147, 153

    "Eclogue the First: Selim; or, The Shepherd's Moral," 91-92

    "Eclogue the Second: Hassan; or, The Camel-Driver," 30, 92-93

    "Eclogue the Third: Abra; or, The Georgian Sultana," 93

    "Eclogue the Fourth: Agib and Secander; or The Fugitives," 92, 93-94

A Review of the Advancement of Learning from 1300 to 1521, 34, 36, 38, 47, 48

"A Song from Shakespeare's *Cymbeline,*" 32, 49, 97-98, 154

"Song" (Young Damon of the vale is dead), 24, 25

"Sonnet" (When *Phœbe* formed a wanton smile), 25-26, 87-89, 98

"To Miss Aurelia C—r," 24

translation of Aristotle's *Poetics,* 32, 40-41, 43, 48, 98

Verses Humbly Address'd to Sir Thomas Hanmer, 31-32, 87, 91, 94-97, 98, 143, 149, 153

"Written in the Beginning of the Year 1746" (How Sleep the Brave), 70, 99, 108-10, 111, 112, 119, 127, 138, 145, 155, 165

"Written on a Paper which contained a Piece of Bride Cake," 24-25

Congreve, William, 67

Cooper, John Gilbert, 47, 48, 50, 65-66, 74, 149; *Letters Concerning Taste*, 47, 74

Correggio, 58

Cowley, Abraham, 130

Cox, H. S., 50

Crabbe, George, 159

Crypt, The, 24

Cumberland, William, duke of, 112

Cunningham, J. S., 95

Cynewulf, 57

Dante, 58

Delacroix, Ferdinand, 111

Dickens, Charles, 132-33; *Great Expectations*, 132-33

Dodsley, Robert, 44, 45, 46, 48, 49, 75, 95, 99, 111, 125, 155; *A Collection of Poems . . . by Several Hands*, 48, 95, 111, 155; *The Museum*, 44, 46, 47; *The Preceptor*, 48, 75

Donne, John, 82

Dryden, John, 58, 60, 61, 63, 64, 67, 81, 82, 85, 134, 153; "Alexander's Feast," 78, 134; *MacFlecknoe*, 142; translation of Horace, 64

Duff, William, 67, 68, 76-77

Dyce, Rev. Alexander, 160

Dyer, John, 64, 66, 67, 78, 160; "The Fleece," 64; "Grongar Hill," 66-67

Eliot, T. S., 70

Emerson, Ralph Waldo, 58

Euripides, 101

Fairfax, Edward, 50, 153; translation of Tasso, 153

Fawkes, Francis, 17, 155; *Poetical Calendar*, 17-18, 155

Foote, Samuel, 37

Frost, Robert, 60

Garrick, David, 36, 37

Garrod, H. W., 99, 100, 136

General Advertiser, The, 50

Genesis, 53

Gentleman's Magazine, The, 21, 24, 25, 31, 46, 49, 156

George I, 32

Gibbon, Edward, 28

Ginsberg, Allen, 59, 70; *Howl*, 70

Glover, Richard, 75; *Leonidas*, 75

Goddard, Miss Elizabeth, 44, 45, 110-11

Goldsmith, Oliver, 18, 89, 93

Goulston, Theodore, 100

Grainger, James, 64; "Sugar-Cane," 64

Gray, Thomas, 23, 65, 67, 78, 81, 84, 93, 95, 112, 119, 135, 150, 156, 157-58, 159, 161, 162, 164; "The Bard," 157, 161; *Elegy Written in a Country Churchyard*, 93, 119, 156, 157-58; "The Fatal Sisters," 157, 158; "Progress of Poesy," 95

Green, Richard, 35, 36

Hammond, James, 18; *Elegies*, 18

Hampton, James, 20

Hanmer, Sir Thomas, 32, 97

Hardham, John, 35, 36, 37

Hardy, Thomas, 58

Hargrave, Captain, 34, 37, 38, 55

Hawley, General, 39

Hay, Alexander, 35, 36, 37, 42; *History of Chichester*, 35, 170

Hayes, Dr. William, 51, 133, 134

Hazlitt, William, 17, 162

Herbert, George, 159

Home, John, 48, 50, 138, 139, 140, 143, 144; *Douglas*, 138

Homer, 20, 63, 64, 74, 142; *Iliad*, 61

Horace, 61, 63, 64, 81, 124, 125, 154, 155, 158

Hume, David, 76

Hunt, Leigh, 162; *Autobiography,* 162

Hymers, William, 30, 169

Johnson, Samuel, 17, 18, 25, 26, 27, 32, 33, 38, 39, 40, 42, 48, 52, 53-54, 54-55, 56, 60, 62, 71, 78, 85, 91, 97, 132, 138, 140, 155, 156, 159; "Life" of Collins, 17, 32-33, 54-55, 85, 138, 147; *Lives of the English Poets,* 24, 62, 159

Juvenal, 63

Keats, John, 67, 123, 140, 143, 145, 159, 162, 163-64, 165; "Ode on a Grecian Urn," 146; "Ode to a Nightingale," 123; "Ode to Autumn," 163

"Kinds" of poetry in the age, 60-64

Langhorne, John, 18, 28, 40, 49, 99, 106, 132, 156

Lecky, W. E. H., 112

Lewis, David, 66; *Miscellaneous Poems,* 66

A Literary Journal, 38

Locke, John, 92

Longinus, 68

Lovelace, Richard, 159-60

Lowell, James Russell, 140

Mackail, J. W., 91

Mackenzie, Henry, 139; *The Man of Feeling,* 139

Manby, J., 35, 39, 41, 50; *Biographia Britannica,* 35, 41

Martin, Colonel Edmund, 31, 35, 36, 39, 41, 42, 46, 48, 49

Martin, Martin, 143, 144; *A Description of the Western Isles of Scotland, Circa 1695,* 143

Mawson, Dr. (Bp. of Chichester), 35

Millar, Andrew, 46, 49, 99

Milton, John, 59, 63, 64, 68, 81, 100, 103, 105, 107-8, 110, 113, 118, 123, 124, 128, 135, 152, 153, 155, 161; "Il Penseroso," 103; "L' Allegro,"

66, 103; *Lycidas,* 118, 136, 137; "Nativity Ode," 105; *Paradise Lost,* 63, 68, 110; *Paradise Regained,* 110; translation of Horace, 124

Milton, William, 43

Miscellaneous Poems and Translations (1726), 66

Monthly Review, 85

Moschus, 23

Mulso, Rev. John, 20, 27, 33, 34, 37, 38, 41, 42, 43, 45, 46

Murdoch, Patrick, 48

Murry, John Middleton, 25-26, 118, 148

Museum, The (Dodsley), 44, 46, 47

Musgrove, S., 100, 134-35

Ogilvie, John, 72-73

Otway, Thomas, 101

Ovid, 66

Oxford English Dictionary, 88, 138

Payne, George, 33, 40, 49

Payne, William, 27, 31, 34, 43

Pemberton, Henry, 75

Personification and Prosopopoeia, 70-77

Petrarch, 58, 59

Phelps, William Lyon, 63

Pindar, 65, 155

Pindarick Ode, characteristics of, 65-67, 70, 106

Plato, 107, 115, 116, 149, 150

Poetic Diction, 78-85

Poetical Calendar, 17-18, 155, 167

Poetry of the Age, 57-85; *see also:* "Kinds" of poetry; Poetic Diction; Personification and Prosopopoeia; Pindarick Ode; Sublimity

Pope, Alexander, 26, 58, 59, 60, 61-63, 78, 81, 82-83, 85, 89, 91, 95, 122, 128, 130, 135, 145, 148, 149, 153, 159, 160; *Dunciad,* 62; "Elegy to an Unfortunate Lady," 82; "Epistle to Arbuthnot," 146; *Essay on Criticism,* 61-62, 63; "Ode for Music on St. Cecilia's Day," 78;

Pastorals, 78, 83, 89; translation of *Iliad,* 61; *Windsor Forest,* 78
Poussin, Nicolas, 97
Preceptor, The (Dodsley), 48, 75
Prior, Matthew, 153

Quin, James, 37
Quintilian, 75

Ragsdale, John, 30-31, 33-34, 35, 37, 40, 41, 45, 129
Ramsay, Allan, 58-59, 62, 66
Raphael, Sanzio, 58
Reynolds, Sir Joshua, 37
Richardson, Samuel, 92; *Letters,* 92
Richmond, Charles Lennox, duke of, 35, 36, 39, 42
Robinson, Henry Crabb, 156
Robinson, Thomas, 156
Rosa, Salvatore, 127
Ross, Captain Charles, 45, 110, 111
Royal Society, 59, 139
Ruysdael, Jacob, 127

Salmon, Thomas, 89, 90-91, 93; *Modern History,* 89; *The Present State of Proper India,* 93
Savage, Richard, 66; *Miscellaneous Poems and Translations,* 66
Schiller, Friedrich, 161
Shaftesbury, Anthony Ashley Cooper, 3d earl of, 149
Shakespeare, William, 21, 32, 59, 81, 86, 96, 97, 98, 102, 103, 129, 135, 141, 142, 145, 152, 153, 155, 161, 165; *Cymbeline,* 97; *A Midsummer Night's Dream,* 21; *Othello,* 59
Shelley, Percy Bysshe, 58, 119, 159; *Adonais,* 137
Shenton, Rev., 53
Shentstone, William, 147
Shuster, George N., 163
Sidney, Sir Philip, 59
Smith, Charlotte, 159
Socrates, 47
Sophocles, 102, 104
Spectator, The, 65, 71

Spence, Joseph, 75-76, 150
Spenser, Edmund, 23, 59, 94, 107, 117, 118, 124, 149, 153; *Faerie Queene,* 71, 107; *Shepheardes Calendar,* 94
Stuart, Charles Edward, 41, 45, 109
Sublimity, concept of, 68-70
Swinburne, Algernon, 156-57
Sypher, Wylie, 150-51

Tasso, 50, 141, 153
Tennyson, Alfred, Lord, 58
Thomas, Dylan, 58, 60, 145; "The Force that through the Green Fuse Drives the Flower," 146
Thomas, W. Moy, 20
Thomson, J. A. K., 154
Thomson, James, 40, 41, 43, 48, 61, 63, 84, 118, 136, 137, 138, 153, 159, 160, 164; *Castle of Indolence,* 136; *Liberty,* 118, 136; *The Seasons,* 79; *Winter,* 63
Thoreau, Henry David, 50
Tillotson, Geoffrey, 78
Tillyard, E. M. W., 138
Times Literary Supplement, 59
Tomkyns, 25; "Beauty and Innocence," 25

Vaughan, Henry, 159
Virgil, 20, 63, 64, 68, 74, 81, 89, 154; *Aeneid,* 64; *Georgics,* 64, 68, 74; *Pastorals,* 64

Waller, Edmund, 59
Walpole, Horace, 144; *Castle of Otranto,* 144
Warton, Joseph, 18, 20, 21, 22, 23, 25, 26, 27, 44, 45, 46, 57, 59, 62, 64, 65, 73-74, 81-82, 88, 89, 99, 102, 108, 110, 117, 124, 138, 140, 153, 158; *Odes on Several Subjects,* 46, 62; *The Temple of Pity,* 102; translation of Horace, 64, 81-82, 125
Warton, Thomas, 17, 18, 21, 24, 33, 38, 44, 45, 47, 48, 52, 53, 102, 111,

117, 138, 140, 153, 154; *History of English Poetry*, 18

Warton, Thomas, the Elder, 21-23, 63, 124, 140; "Ode on Taste," 23, 124

Wasserman, Earl R., 76

West, Richard, 81

White, Gilbert, 17, 29, 33, 34, 37, 38, 45, 47, 48, 52, 55-56, 133

White, H. O., 27

Whitehall Evening Post, 50

Whitehead, William, 20

Woodhouse, A. S. P., 149

Wooll, John, 25, 168

Wordsworth, William, 24, 58, 70, 78, 79, 80, 81, 99, 120, 128, 149, 156, 159, 160, 161; *Lyrical Ballads*, 135; "Remembrance of Collins," 160; "Tintern Abbey," 70

Woty, William, 17-18, 155; *Poetical Calendar*, 17-18, 155

Young, Edward, 110, 153; *Night Thoughts*, 153